etic call to remember that our worth as women, as survivors, can never be taken from us. Our worth is right here for us to reclaim, from within. Brooke Axtell's story of healing her trauma, returning to her body, and finding fierce love for herself leads to the greatest triumph of all, to the light no darkness can extinguish; the voice of her own soul."

—Meggan Watterson, author of *Reveal* and *The Sutras of Unspeakable Joy* and coauthor of *How to Love Yourself*

"*Beautiful Justice* is a fierce declaration of survival, grace, and dignity. Axtell bares her soul to the world in searing prose that demands we hear the voices of survivors with respect and compassion. Her perseverance in the face of brutality reminds us of all that is noble in the human spirit."

—Siddharth Kara, author of *Modern Slavery: A Global Perspective* and *Sex Trafficking: Inside the Business of Modern Slavery*

"*Beautiful Justice* lives up to its name. Brooke Axtell's beautifully written story is born of personal tragedy and triumph. Told with warmth, humor, and pride, [Axtell] shares lessons we can all learn from."   —Terry Lickona, coproducer of The Grammy Awards

"Brooke Axtell's genius book *Beautiful Justice* proves that every woman has a story that deserves to be heard, and no matter its contents, can be transformed. You will find your story in hers. You'll be reminded that we can all play a part to create a world where women are valued."   —Gina DeVee, creator of Divine Living

"*Beautiful Justice* perfectly describes Brooke Axtell's deeply compelling book. Her poetry weaves her personal story of abuse and child sex trafficking through her own heroine's journey to healing. She reveals how she turned the pain of her trauma into passion for social justice. And she offers a handbook for sexual abuse survivors (and, frankly, all women), gently coaching us to reclaim our bodies, our voices, and our power to lead and live as we freely choose."

—Gloria Feldt, cofounder and president
of Take the Lead and author of *No Excuses:*
9 Ways Women Can Change How We Think About Power

"As a survivor of sexual exploitation and abuse, Brooke Axtell takes us on her journey with painstaking honesty and integrity. She takes the reader through her music and poetry and shows us how strong the spirit is. We intimately meet the girl, the woman, the survivor, the advocate, the artist, as she inspires others to their healing. Brooke is an inspiration to all sexual abuse survivors, and as she eloquently writes, 'The pain we feel is not infinite. Love is.' There is a lot of love in *Beautiful Justice*."

—Dr. Patti Feuereisen, founder of Girlthrive
and author of *Invisible Girls: Speaking the*
Truth About Sexual Abuse

"In her reclamation of worth, Brooke is a beacon. A white-hot burning flame of truth. The words and wisdom held within this book are fierce and much-needed medicine for these times."

—Lisa Lister, author of *Witch* and *Love Your Lady Landscape*

"Axtell plumbs the horrors of her trauma as a poet, bard, seeker, and seer and establishes herself firmly as a moral and spiritual authority—and, endearingly, as a teacher and as a friend....It is in fact Axtell's unflinching candor that allows the reader to grasp the full extent of trauma and the turbulence of the healing journey. Axtell assumes nothing and therefore reveals everything. If one ever doubts the importance of artists and authors to serve as moral beacons for society, let them read this exceptional book."

—Sanjay Rawal, award-winning documentary filmmaker and activist

"Axtell [is] an example of the power in speaking out."

—*Rolling Stone*

"A powerful voice." —*Austin-American Statesman*

"Brooke is a multitalented, inspiring, and impressive woman. A rising star." —Debra Condren, bestselling author of *Ambition Is Not a Dirty Word*

"Brooke is a dynamic young force."

—Suzy Spencer, *New York Times*–bestselling author of *Wasted*

"In Brooke Axtell's stunning book of fierce love, fierce devotion, and fierce healing, she shares her personal journey through abuse, step by step, and integrates it into a road map for others. She honors the many different paths of a woman's spiritual and psychological inner terrain and affirms there are as many paths as there are women. Brooke generously reveals the way art healed her life and in turn shows us the way to do the same with our own."

—Deborah Kampmeier, filmmaker and director of *Hounddog* and *Split*

Beautiful Justice

Reclaiming My Worth
After Human Trafficking
and Sexual Abuse

Brooke Axtell

SEAL
PRESS

Seal Press
Hachette Book Group
1290 Avenue of the Americas, New York, NY 10104
@sealpress
Sealpress.com

Printed in the United States of America

First Edition: April 2019

Published by Seal Press, an imprint of Perseus Books, LLC, a subsidiary of Hachette Book Group, Inc. The Seal Press name and logo is a trademark of the Hachette Book Group.

The Hachette Speakers Bureau provides a wide range of authors for speaking events. To find out more, go to www.hachettespeakersbureau.com or call (866) 376-6591.

The publisher is not responsible for websites (or their content) that are not owned by the publisher.

Print book interior design by Six Red Marbles Inc.

Library of Congress Cataloging-in-Publication Data has been applied for.

ISBNs: 978-1-58005-824-7 (paperback), 978-1-58005-825-4 (ebook)

LSC-C

10 9 8 7 6 5 4 3 2 1

This is for my sisters who survived.
This is for my sisters who never made it out alive
to find voice lessons.
This is for my sisters who are denied
the birthright of freedom.
You are not alone.
I have not forgotten you.

Contents

v

Contents

You can't keep fire in a cage.
You can't keep the wind in chains.
What is true cannot be tamed.
The falling tide will rise again.
I have danced with the hurricane.
I have kissed the mouth of thunder.
I reach for the lightning
when everyone runs for cover.
Dare you come closer?
Closer you will find:
I am the wild kind.

An Invitation to Beautiful Justice

WELCOME. Thank you for being here.

This book is my offering to you.

I write these words in honor of survivors and their allies.

Survivors of sexual assault, domestic violence, and human trafficking. Survivors of childhood abuse and neglect. Survivors of emotional abuse, sexual harassment, and exploitation. Survivors who know what it feels like to be violated, devalued, and cast aside.

I share my story of overcoming abuse and finding emotional freedom to encourage you to step into your own. I believe you are worth fighting for. No matter what trauma you may have experienced, I want you to know healing is possible for you.

In this book, you will discover how I healed from child sex trafficking, sexual assault, and domestic violence to become a leader in the international movement for human rights. At the end of the story, you will also find what I call "soul medicine," encouragement and guidance for your unique path to Beautiful Justice.

Beautiful Justice is the art of taking back our lives and reclaiming our worth after abuse. It is a form of justice that does not depend on what happens to our perpetrators. It is centered on our recovery as a creative process.

Beautiful Justice honors our resilience and agency.

We don't have to wait for someone else's choices to set us free. Every decision we make as survivors to speak our truth, reclaim our worth, name our desires, and step into our dreams is a powerful expression of justice that must be celebrated.

I believe survivors have a right to redefine what justice means to them outside of the criminal justice system. I am passionate about creating a more expansive and life-giving view of justice that centers on survivor voices and choices rather than a model that reduces justice to punishing a perpetrator for a crime.

Of course, accountability for perpetrators is needed, but in a world where the vast majority of rapists and abusers will never spend a day in jail, we are creating our own justice by cultivating ways to thrive, awakening our deep resilience, and emerging as leaders. We don't have to wait for someone to be imprisoned in order to finally feel free.

One definition of justice is "the quality of being just." An exploration of the word *just* reveals a meaning that is powerfully relevant for survivors of abuse. One meaning is this: "what is deserved." When we consider what is deserved after an incident of abuse, we often focus on what we believe the abuser deserves.

But what about survivors? What do *we* deserve?

In the aftermath of physical and emotional violence, how should our communities respond to *us*?

As a survivor, I do not want to be reduced to someone else's criminal act. I want my creative power to be seen and acknowledged as more important and vital than what was forced on my body. Beautiful Justice means I don't have to wait for a power outside myself to finally tell me I am worthy.

Beautiful Justice is the integration of inner healing and cultural healing, recovery of the individual, and the movement for social change. It can include a survivor's choice to press charges against a perpetrator (in her own time, for her own reasons), but it does not depend on this.

Beautiful Justice is a return to our innate wholeness. It is the remembrance of our power. It is the path of transforming pain into fierce wisdom, wisdom that can ultimately help heal our communities.

Beautiful Justice also includes our deeply intimate and personal definitions of what it means to live a beautiful life. I marry beauty with justice in my vision of recovery because beauty signals that we are moving beyond mere survival into abundance.

When I consider the places and people that have been most nurturing for me, I see irresistible beauty: captivating art, the wild grace of nature, the luminosity of a soul devoted to a path of love.

In a world where the criminal justice system often fails us, we still have the power to create our own justice. For instance, although approximately one in six women will be sexually assaulted, more than 90 percent of rapists will never spend a day in jail.

And in the rare instance that the criminal justice system effectively convicts the perpetrator and protects a crime victim, justice is often incomplete because incarcerating an abuser does not set a survivor free from the impact of the trauma.

If a young trafficked girl sees her trafficker sentenced to prison, yet she lives with a relentless sense of shame and wakes up feeling worthless, that is not justice. If she still feels compelled to tolerate abusive behavior from men in order to win their approval, that is not justice. If she feels the only way out of her pain is drug and alcohol abuse, that is not justice. If she feels her only value is her sexuality and the ways she can please men, that is not justice.

It is not *just* because it is not *what she deserves*. She deserves to know her worth.

That is why, even when perpetrators are held accountable for their actions, we still need a more expansive view of justice. We need a justice that includes the emotional freedom of those who have endured abuse and exploitation.

In the course of this book, I am redefining justice to include and honor our well-being as survivors. As we take back our power and reclaim our worth, we are stepping into Beautiful Justice. We are no longer waiting for someone else to set us free.

The trauma of abuse ruptures our connection to our sense of worth. But our worth is unconditional. Beautiful Justice is the way to reconnect with that unwavering worth.

The pain we feel is not infinite. Love is.

And love invites us to relinquish all the lies we have been told about who we are, so we can come home to our wholeness. By devoting ourselves to this healing path, we make the world a more just and compassionate place.

I have seen the ravages of justice denied, and it is time for us to create our own justice, to define our own vision of what it means to honor our worth.

What does a survivor of abuse deserve?
We deserve . . .

to be heard
to be supported
to be believed
to be celebrated
to be loved unconditionally by our communities.

Our tenderness is strength. Our bliss is a form of resistance. Our self-compassion is revolutionary. Our pleasure is lifesaving. Our humanity is undeniable. Our collective hope is intoxicating.

A NOTE TO ALLIES

If you are reading this book as an ally to survivors of abuse, you, too, can be a part of creating Beautiful Justice. Here are ways to begin:

1. Survivors are told they are worthless. Affirm our worth with your actions and words.
2. Survivors are taught their desires do not matter. Encourage us to explore and honor our desires. Support us in practical ways to manifest our dreams.
3. Survivors are treated with contempt. Offer us compassion.
4. Survivors feel isolated and alone. Invite us into your circle, your family, your heart, your home. Keep reaching out.
5. Survivors fear the pain will never pass. Remind us of our joy.

6. Survivors feel silenced and ashamed. Remind us our voices matter. Listen deeply when we share our stories and heal your own shame, so you can walk this path of recovery with us.
7. Survivors often blame themselves for the abuse. Remind us it is not our fault and we are worthy of love.

When you don't know what to say, you can say this: "I am sorry you are hurting. I am here."

You can ask these simple, yet powerful, questions:

What do you want?

What do you need?

How can I support you?

What would feel comforting right now?

What is one way you can be kind to yourself today?

What is the truth you need to tell?

Together we are creating Beautiful Justice. With each small act of compassion, we are mending a brokenhearted world.

Welcome home.

In Fierce Love,

Brooke Axtell

PART ONE

What the Fire Sang to Me

chapter one

Worthy of Love

A S I STEP ONTO THE STAGE of the Grammys, I hear the voice of President Obama, telling the world that violence against women and girls must end. "It's on us," he says with quiet confidence and conviction. His words resound through my body as I walk forward in the dark.

Then the spotlight hits me. The rows close to the stage are illuminated. I see pop music icon and sexual assault survivor Madonna.

"How many of us have remained silent for years, bound by shame?" I wonder.

When my time to speak comes, I pray to be a channel of healing and liberation for those experiencing abuse. Peace envelops me. "My name is Brooke Axtell, and I am a survivor of domestic violence. After a year of passionate romance with a handsome, charismatic man, I was stunned when he began to abuse me.

"I wanted to believe he was lashing out because he was in pain and needed help. I wanted to believe my compassion could restore him and our relationship. My empathy was used against me. My compassion was incomplete because it did not include me.

"When he threatened to kill me, I knew I had to escape. I revealed the truth of my relationship to my mom, and she encouraged me to seek help at a local domestic violence shelter. This conversation saved my life."

I feel my power returning to me. I am not afraid anymore.

"If you are in a relationship with someone who does not honor and respect you, I want you to know you are worthy of love. Please reach out for help. Your voice will save you. Let it extend into the night. Let it part the darkness. Let it set you free to know who you truly are: valuable, beautiful, loved."

After I finish my last line, Katy Perry sings "By the Grace of God." Her voice resonates with beautiful clarity. "By the grace of God, I picked myself back up." There is strength in her vulnerability.

I descend the stairs backstage and see Annie Lennox coming toward me. She has tears in her eyes and says, "You are wonderful." As she embraces me in a warm hug, my heart floods with gratitude. I am overwhelmed by her kindness.

It took me so long to view myself with empathy and respect, but tonight I cross a threshold in my healing and freedom. I recognize I have finally learned to value my own voice.

As I make my way back to my seat in the audience beside my mother, I think of all my survivor sisters and our allies who are devoted to the undeniable worth of women and girls. I feel them walking with me. I hear women's voices once buried by violence shake the earth beneath me and harmonize.

Together we are untamed light. My whole body vibrates with the knowledge of our collective power: to heal, liberate, and bring an end to the cycle of violence and oppression.

When I return to my seat, I talk with film director Ava DuVernay. She is here to watch Beyoncé, Common, and John Legend perform the song "Glory" from her film *Selma*.

"You are *fabulous*," she says.

I am in awe she is acknowledging me.

"Thank you. So are *you*," I reply.

Surrounded by influential celebrities and producers in the entertainment industry, Ava generously takes a moment to encourage me. She has nothing to gain from speaking to me, so I deeply appreciate her authenticity and grace.

I tell her how much I love her film and how important Dr. King's work is for me as a human rights activist. When Beyoncé performs "Glory," chills rush through my body. It has always been my dream to be a part of the legacy of freedom fighters. Yet I lived for many years not knowing whether I would ever find the emotional and spiritual freedom I deeply craved.

I consider all I have overcome to reach this moment as well as the stories of the abused women and girls I carry with me. The stories of those who survived and the stories of those who never made it out alive. Draped in a black sequined evening gown, I have shared an extremely concise account of the abuse I survived as an adult. But I could not convey in only a couple of minutes how brutal the darkness was before I reached the first glimpse of light.

Though flooded with gratitude to be here, even during this night of celebration, so many are still trapped in abusive relationships and disconnected from the birthright of their worth.

BEFORE I EVEN return to the hotel, I receive messages from women across the country telling me how powerfully my story speaks to them. Women reveal how they had been beaten, shot, run over by cars, verbally abused, and demeaned by their husbands and boyfriends, men who claimed to love them. Some send photographs of their beaten faces. Daughters write to tell me how their mothers and sisters were murdered.

The next morning I give an interview on *Access Hollywood*. A man who works for the show approaches me and says, "I heard your speech last night, and it meant a lot to me. I went through an abusive relationship, too. It wasn't physical. It was emotional."

"I am sorry to hear that," I say. "Thank you for sharing your story with me. Many survivors say emotional abuse is the worst part."

In the following days, I also receive stories of resilience. Women decide to leave abusive relationships after hearing my speech and start their healing path. Many of them say they related to what I shared about my empathy being used against me. In all these messages I hear a common refrain, "My compassion did not include me."

One of the most moving responses comes from a fifteen-year-old girl, a courageous poet and survivor of sex trafficking. A few weeks after the Grammys, I speak to her recovery group for survivors of child sex trafficking in Miami. The girls ask me questions about my own recovery.

Then the young poet says, "I really related to your speech."

"What part resonated with you the most?" I ask.

"The part when you said, 'I am worthy of love.'"

Later that night, I receive a photograph of a journal entry she wrote in response to our conversation. She says, "As I learned tonight, it's very important to have hope. It's important to have someone, anyone, who cares. No matter what people may say or do to you, it's important to never give up. I believe faith with the right help can go a long way. And you're not going to change overnight. It takes time and there is nothing wrong with that. I learned tonight that I am worth something and that I am made for greatness."

This is why I continue my work as an advocate and human rights leader with gratitude and hope. In the face of such darkness, I see survivors rise up with the knowledge of their worth, and it is magnificent.

Another teenage survivor of sex trafficking asks me, "After everything you went through as a child, how can you still have hope? How did you get to where you are?"

"The healing path is difficult," I say. "But you are worth fighting for. Never give up. Be patient with yourself. Reach out for the help you need. Surround yourself with people who see how valuable you are and will remind you of the truth when you can't believe it for yourself."

Her question brings me back to the beginning, to the first time a man told me I had no worth, to the first time I was sold for sex.

chapter two

Underworld Girl

I AM SEVEN YEARS OLD, and my favorite color is pink. I love ballet. Books, dolls, and art fill my room. I read for hours on my white chaise surrounded by stuffed animals and listen to my music box with the delicate roses and gold edges. My dream is to become a writer one day.

I love to sing "Castle on a Cloud" from the musical *Les Misérables*. The young Cosette, separated from her mother and condemned to a life of abuse, cries out, "I know a place where no one is lost. I know a place where no one cries. Crying at all is not allowed. Not in my castle on a cloud."

My teachers at school tell me to stop sucking my thumb. "Big girls don't suck their thumbs," they say. What do *they* know? They do not see what I see. This is how I comfort myself, and I won't give it up. I stop sucking my thumb at school but continue at home. It helps me fall asleep at night. It helps me forget.

When I take baths, I rest on my back and sing the first song I created, "Flying wings, angels sing, strawberry dreams." Over and over I sing the same chorus, moving my arms like an angel.

Hanging from the bathroom wall is a framed verse from the book of I Samuel. It is known as Hannah's Prayer, but in this version, my name replaces the name of the son she prays for. The calligraphy reads, "I have prayed for this child, Brooke, and the Lord has granted me what I have asked of him, so now I give her to the Lord. For her whole life she will be given over to him."

My mom taught me God is love. But she is in the hospital now because of a sickness that left her unable to walk or speak. The doctors say she may never walk again. I fear she will never return. My dad travels for work to take care of our family and pay for the expensive hospital bills, so I have a string of nannies. One after another.

The fat Irish woman who left us in the house alone and told us it was "hide and go seek." The lady from India with the scarred face who stole my mom's credit card and showed us a movie about strippers. The sensitive Polish woman, whose husband painted landscapes with prize racehorses. The baton twirler from Iowa.

The two women from Ethiopia who smiled sweetly and made rich, spicy food, traditional dishes from their homeland. The joyful woman named Dee Dee, who had a thick braid of blonde hair falling down to her lower back and later married a man named Dee.

The studious woman with wiry hair, a mouse face, and glasses who wrapped a towel around me when I got out of the tub. I loved the African ladies most. One of them slept in my pink room for a while. She smelled like red spices and shea-butter body cream.

My nanny now is a man who says he serves God. Jack wears baseball caps and plaid shirts. He plays video games and refuses to wash the dishes. My nanny talks about God, too. He says it is God's will for him to punish me for my sins.

What punishment do I deserve? He does not say the word, and I do not have language for what is happening. I cannot tell anyone what his deity demands on my white iron bed with the pink sheets. "You are a worthless whore," he tells me. "You make me do this to you." When he hurts me, repeating the Lord's Prayer, I fly outside my body.

His voice echoes within me: "Deliver us from evil. Deliver us from evil." A part of me splits off to survive, to guard the truth, to carry the unbearable weight of this. I multiply and disappear.

The first time he hurts me, a door opens into his underworld. A place filled with secrets and shadows, people with dead eyes. He secretly takes me to houses and parties to sell me to men for sex.

They film me with adults and other children. I am caged and taunted like a trapped animal. This all happens in one of the most affluent areas of Texas, Highland Park, in Dallas, where families live and play on idyllic oak-lined streets laced with luxury cars and sprawling mansions.

When they film me, I fly outside my body to take refuge in the beautiful worlds I create: one with a white horse, one where I dance with the angels. Each time they invade me, I soar above them.

I am passed from man to man, hand to hand, like a disposable doll. My soul travels and retreats, crosses oceans, centuries. I live a thousand lives in a single night. Imagination is my fortress.

Reality is unbearable, so I create my own.

This rhythm continues. During the day, I attend school. At night, I belong to him—and whoever is interested in buying me. The buyers are wealthy white men who are hungry to inflict pain. Some of the most painful moments occur when I am forced to watch others being abused.

I numb myself, circling my life as if it belongs to someone else. I became a watcher of the abuse. This is happening to some other little girl, the evil one who needs to be punished, I tell myself. I create a wall, so I can live on the light side and be the good one who lives without pain.

But I cannot fully escape this torment. It bleeds into my writing and art. When I visit my mom in the hospital, she looks like a pale mannequin in her white gown, surrounded by tubes. I don't know what to say, so I give her a poem I wrote about a baby lamb that is separated from her flock. She encourages me to read my poem aloud.

LOST
Over the steep hill
Under a bright horizon
A small lamb lay in a soft green pasture
All alone and full of fright
With wandering eyes
It searches for its flock
But is overcome
by darkness.

My brothers laugh when I reach the part about the fear, so I crawl under a table to hide while the nurse comes in to tend to my mom. "How are you?" the nurse asks warmly. "I read a poem," I reply, as if that explains everything. What I do not say is this: I am afraid. I am afraid I am going to lose her. I am afraid she will stay like this and never come home.

But after a month of treatment and physical therapy, my mom does return home from the hospital in a wheelchair. She is still unable to speak, but she writes notes to me, saying, "I love you." "I love you," I write back. "You can talk," she writes on a small piece of paper. But I don't want to talk. I am too terrified and ashamed. My mom senses something is wrong, though, and fires my nanny.

*W*ITH BOTH MY parents finally home, I return to the comfort of family dinners, laughter, and music. When my dad is in town, he plays guitar for us and sings silly songs as I dance around the living room with my brothers, Luke and Cliff. He rewrites the lyrics to fifties and sixties tunes, so each one of us has a theme song to dance to. My theme song is called "Brookie Boo," which is a rewrite of the Buddy Holly classic "Peggy Sue." Every time he starts the song "Brookie Boo, I love you," I giggle and prance around the room.

My dad also creates a series of adventure stories called "Sissy and Bubba." This courageous brother-and-sister duo travel, on their own, to places like the Amazon jungle and Siberia in hot air balloons on undercover missions and overcome countless villains all before their bedtime.

My older brother, Luke, is tall, quiet, and a keen observer of everyone around him. He lives for his time in nature: exploring creeks, fishing, and collecting insects and turtles. Strong yet tenderhearted, Luke exudes a steadfast loyalty.

He doesn't say much, but fights for those he loves. When one of the cruel neighborhood boys tries to bully me, he stands up to him until he finally backs down. "Leave my sister alone," Luke demands, clenching his fists. When the same pudgy black-haired boy tries to attack our soft-spoken Polish nanny, Luke stares him down and punches him in the face without saying a word.

My younger brother, Clifton, loves to express himself, radiates passion, and always finds some kind of mischief. He bolted out of the house at the age of three and furiously pedaled his Big Wheel down the street, completely naked. He is endlessly curious and wants to know how everything works. We call Clifton "Day Day" because before he could talk, he would wander around the house repeating the word *day, day, day, day*.

My dad makes me laugh again. Blaring Led Zeppelin in the car, he does his weird car dance where he pumps his fist in the air as we both sing along with Robert Plant. He plays his favorite classic rock records for me and introduces me to artists like Moody Blues, Jethro Tull, and Crosby, Stills, Nash & Young.

Dad also takes me out to eat at my favorite Mexican food restaurant and treats me to trips to the local book and music stores, telling me I can pick out any book or CD I want. "Always remember," he says as we browse adventure stories and fairy tales, "books are our friends. Readers are leaders."

I smile, indulging him. "I know, Dad."

He takes me to art museums, concerts, and Broadway musicals. For my first concert, my mom, dad, brothers, and I go to see the Beach Boys. I adore their music and dance the whole afternoon beside my father, wearing my new pair of white sunglasses. He reminds me joy is still possible.

With all the demands of his travel, providing for our family, and taking care of my mom, my dad notices no signs of the abuse. My parents think my sadness is due to the pain of having been separated from my mom and her struggle with severe health issues. I only want to please him and make him proud of me.

One of Dad's nicknames for me is "Ferocious Brain." He walks into the kitchen in the morning and pats me on the head, saying, "How is my Ferocious Brain doing today?" He affirms my intellect, my ability to think for myself, and often plays devil's advocate, so I have to defend my point of view.

Although he does not know about my trauma, he offers a different story to the one forced on me by my trafficker. My dad teaches me that my mind matters. In the aftermath of being treated like an object, he tells me, "You are formidable."

During this time, my mom devotes herself to the demanding routines of continuous physical therapy and gradually transitions to a walker. She refuses to accept the doctors' suggestions that she should accept her lack of mobility. With a dedicated therapist who works with her in the water, my mom learns to walk again, and her speech slowly begins to return.

REUNITED WITH MY mom, I feel safe and nurtured. The abuse is a film I place in a vault and lock up far away. She is with me now. Nothing else matters. There is no need to confess. It is over.

I tell myself, "It never happened."

The good girl I create, the one who always lives in the light, the one who was never abused, takes over my life. She excels in every way. I lose myself in ballet, the demands of rigorous elegance, where my body is my own. I perform in professional productions with the Dallas Ballet and find strength in the discipline of each graceful movement.

I love the sound of live grand piano reverberating through our downtown studio. The black floors, large windows opening to the city skyline, the wall of mirrors, amber rosin, black leotards, and soft pink tights create a sense of order and safety for me. This is my refuge. I dance as if they never touched me.

I tell myself, "They never touched me."

I master the art of forgetting. I dwell in imagination. The girl who was hurt does not live here anymore. I study the Bible my parents gave me and search the Scriptures for truth. I am hungry for wisdom and want to understand the nature of God. I discover insights in Proverbs and passion in the Psalms. I find solace there.

One of the verses I carry with me is "Let them praise His name with dancing." I know the Divine inside the dancing. That is enough for me. I am a little budding mystic.

I do not feel at home at church, but I am passionately devoted to seeking the truth and living in complete union with love. I pray often and sing to the angels. I love the way Wisdom in Proverbs is portrayed as a woman. I want to be like her.

I underline some of my favorite verses: "She is clothed with strength and dignity. She can laugh at the days to come. She speaks with wisdom and graceful instruction is on her tongue."

I strive for perfection in every dimension of my life—my dance, my studies, my spiritual path. I want to shine so brightly the shadows cannot consume me.

*I*N THIRD GRADE, I approach my teacher, whom I call Dr. G., at the public elementary school and say, "School is not challenging enough for me." He listens thoughtfully, stroking his brown beard, and says, "I understand."

After this conversation, Dr. G. tells me I can start going to the library on my own for an hour during class. "Read whatever you want and write a report on it." I am thrilled. Being left alone to wander the library is heaven for me. I check out several biographies and write papers on historical figures, including Benjamin Franklin and Russian ballerina Anna Pavlova.

My parents talk with him about moving me to a more rigorous school, and he encourages them to apply to Hockaday, a private girls' academy. I am accepted and enroll the following year.

Being surrounded with other bright, curious, driven girls at Hockaday gives me a sense of hope. The classes are advanced, and the culture of the school is highly encouraging and supportive. It is the first time I remember being in an environment where girls' voices and intellectual contributions are fully valued.

For two years, Hockaday is my academic and creative haven. I write poetry, choreograph a couple of dance pieces for performances, study piano and French, write my first speech, and win a speech contest.

Between my studies and my immersion in ballet, I claim a sense of identity for myself. At the age of ten, I am cast in the role of Clara in the *Nutcracker* for the Dallas Ballet. All my focus and dedication led to this moment. I am shocked when I read the cast list, but thrilled to be chosen.

After a couple of years at Hockaday, my family moves north of Houston, and I attend the Houston Ballet Academy. I am taking ballet classes and rehearsing for productions of the *Nutcracker* six days a week.

Aside from school, my world is the world of the ballet. That is where I feel powerful and free. I continue writing poetry, stories, and songs. Creative expression is my spiritual path. It gives me a world to live in, a world of my own creation.

ALTHOUGH THE ABUSE ended suddenly, the shame did not. No matter how much I accomplish in life, I am still vulnerable to falling back into my trafficker's lie about me: "worthless, worthless,

worthless." I live for many years concealing the secret of my trauma. What I witnessed feels unspeakable.

I am deeply invested in striving for perfection. My focus and relentless drive keep me from feeling helpless. My achievements protect me for a time. They serve as a barrier against the helplessness and the haunting sense that there is something wrong with me.

I experience moments of joy with a new accomplishment in my writing, education, or ballet career. Yet it is never enough to bring enduring relief. I win awards, lead roles, and academic honors. But it never sets me free. It is not enough to heal me.

There is sorrow beneath every celebration. Even when I am surrounded by love, I struggle with a penetrating sense of loneliness.

I create connection with others by trying to take care of their needs. This makes me feel less isolated, but I am not fully known. As much as I love my family, I feel I don't belong, because no one can see what is happening inside of me.

My parents care for me and invest in my passions, but they do not recognize how haunted I am. Their commitment to support my creative dreams and academic desires gives me a safe harbor in the midst of my turmoil. But the poison of my abusers seethes just beneath the surface of a perfect performance. I am loved, yet I often feel unloved because my pain is unseen.

My aunt Erin lives on a farm in Hockley, Texas, a rural town close to Houston. I feel safe and nurtured there. Erin, my mom's younger sister, is a light to me. Her blue-green eyes emanate pure compassion, and she has a gift for making everyone around her feel valued.

She always calls me "Boo Boo." Aunt Erin feeds me fresh short-bread still warm from the oven and gives me cappuccinos topped with cinnamon. "Let's make a moment," she says, handing me the homemade treats.

The ryegrass on her land is an emerald green, and I often walk barefoot across the pastures to the horse barn. One day, I walk over to one of her brown quarter horses who is lingering by a wood fence. I stroke his neck and face and whisper to him, "You are so beautiful."

Climbing up to the top of the fence, I hike my leg over his back, hold on to his mane, and give him a slight kick. "Let's go," I urge him. He starts to trot and then releases his majestic body into a full gallop as I keep telling him to go faster. With the warm Texas wind blowing through my long brown hair, I ride bareback to the other side of the field, one with his powerful rhythm, the beat of his hooves striking the earth.

This is what freedom feels like, I think, as the gold and red strokes of sunset spread behind the pine trees.

chapter three

The Artist and the Destroyer

There is a mighty hand
gently igniting my piano keys
Why do you fear the music?
I cannot tell you what I have seen.
To hear you must believe.
I am a woman built of eyes.
Forgive me.

IN MIDDLE SCHOOL, my past surfaces in my poetry and stories. The memories of abuse are locked up in the vault of films inside of me, but the emotional truth and images slip into my writing.

For English class, in eighth grade, I write a poem about a desperate middle-aged drug addict who hallucinates that his drug is speaking to him, saying, "I am your master and you are my slave." In the poem, the addict is ultimately consumed by his craving and sees no way out.

When people ask me, I cannot tell them where this scene came from. As far as anyone can see, I am sheltered from the outside world. I grew up without watching television, and I am surrounded by the culture of conservative Christianity in the South.

In my life on the surface, I have never been exposed to these kinds of stories. This imagery lives inside of me because of what I have already experienced as a child. I understand the mind of a middle-aged addict and emotional slavery of men who pursue their cravings at all cost.

Another poem I write features an elderly woman who has lost all her family members. For a moment, she hallucinates that they have returned to her as she rests by her fire. When they disappear, the disturbed woman cannot bear losing them again, so she runs outside into a brutal winter storm. Seized with delirium, she dances in the snow until she cannot move any longer and freezes to death.

When I sit at my small desk in English class and write my assignments, these are the kinds of poems that flow through me, scenes of madness and despair. The stories are not my own, but they carry emotional truths I need to share.

My short, round teacher with curly gray hair and wire-rimmed glasses assigns Maya Angelou's *I Know Why the Caged Bird Sings*. Reading Angelou's account of her childhood sexual abuse and the loss of her voice makes me feel less alone. The lyrical way she illuminates her pain shows me what is most devastating can be rendered beautiful through writing.

I am not ready to speak about my abuse, but her courage and exquisite skill as storyteller offer a way forward. As Angelou said, "There is no greater agony than bearing an untold story inside of you." Through fictional stories in the form of poetry, I share what I am ready to share, the emotional reality hiding beneath the surface.

I also read the work of Edgar Allan Poe and love the way he played with gothic imagery. There is solace for me in the darkness of his stories. I already feel haunted, so it is a relief to find a language for that haunting.

I CAN MAKE NEW friends and join in conversations at school. I have an instinct for how to speak to people in a way that makes them feel valued. My circle of friends treats me with kindness and appreciates my eccentricities. But I don't feel I can open up about what I actually am feeling and thinking. I feel like an outsider. I am alone even among friends.

At the lunchroom table, they cheerfully chat about boys, clothes, makeup, and what they watched on TV the night before. Since I don't watch TV and I am not interested in middle school boys, I play along, but have little to contribute to the conversation. They make me laugh, and I am glad to have a place to belong, but cannot relate to their world. I have seen too much.

I was already an old soul when I arrived on this earth. My exposure to the underworld of sex trafficking, pornography, religious abuse, and addiction sets me apart as well.

With the absence of sitcoms and teen magazines in my life, I am also cut off from a lot of pop culture. My parents decided not to have those influences in our house because they wanted my creativity to flourish. I don't resist their boundaries because none of it interests me anyway.

I love Stevie Nicks. My friends love the Backstreet Boys. I want to talk about Poe's "Tell-Tale Heart." They talk about *Full House*. While they read *Seventeen*, I read the book of Proverbs. For fun.

They accept me, but sometimes I feel like a ghost, floating around, observing a life that does not make sense to me. I watch and listen carefully. I take notes like a scientist studying a peculiar new species.

I eventually find some girls I can relate to a bit more. When I go over to their houses to hang out, we watch movies like *The Princess Bride* and *So I Married an Axe Murderer*, reciting all the best lines and laughing hysterically. We act in school plays together and talk about saving the whales. Finding a few witty girls who are passionate about art and protecting the environment makes me feel less crazy.

After my mom reads my poetry from class, she decides it's time to take me to my first poetry reading in Houston. I walk into the room clutching my poems and notice most of the writers are middle aged. I am not interested in sharing my poetry with old men in gray beards. But it winds up feeling surprisingly natural, like I am supposed to be here.

I step up to the microphone as though I always do this.

Though I feel resistant to being vulnerable with my work, it also feels instinctual, as if there is nowhere else I should be. I passionately read my poems of madness, addiction, and suicide and realize the poets in the audience are not troubled by what I share.

I can say anything I want to, and it is accepted. After the reading, I talk with one of the older men as we drink stale coffee out of little cups.

"Keep writing," he says.

"I will," I reply, knowing it's true.

The reading shows me there is a community for me. As an eighth-grade girl, I am by far the youngest poet there, but I feel I have found my tribe. My mom intuitively knew I needed to start sharing my poetry, and she was right. I feel I can be myself, talking with these eccentric older writers. They are weird and wise. They recognize me as one of their own.

At another reading, a woman approaches me afterward and says, "When I was your age, I burned all my poetry. Don't burn your poetry."

"I won't," I respond.

I see the sadness in her eyes as if she is still mourning a part of herself she has lost.

ANOTHER OF MY mom's intuitions leads us to Fredericksburg, Texas. Fredericksburg is a small, romantic town known for its peaches, antiques, and bed-and-breakfasts. The main drag has beautiful stone storefronts and a library I adore. It has vaulted ceilings, expansive windows, and a bronze door handle carved with a hummingbird. We travel there for a weekend retreat in a log cabin by a small creek. We write in our journals, drink peach iced tea, and read books on the porch.

One night we stumble onto Hill Top Café for dinner and meet the inspiring owner, blues musician Johnny Nicholas. It is late, and the restaurant is empty except for actress Madeleine Stowe and her party. *The Last of the Mohicans* is one of my favorite movies, and I am mesmerized by her.

She had recently bought a ranch outside of Fredericksburg and asked her friends to join her for dinner, so they could help her name it. After they offer different suggestions, she interrupts and says, "I think we should just call it 'the Lazy Ass.'" They break into laughter as Johnny comes by to wait on us.

Once he takes care of our food and drinks, he sits down to play steel guitar, piano, and harmonica. I listen as his powerful, gritty voice fills the room while savoring the fried green tomatoes he gave me. I feel completely at home in his space, a converted old gas station, covered in hubcaps and vintage blues posters.

Talking to Johnny after his set is another moment of recognition for me. I know he is one of my people. What I don't know is that he is a Grammy Award–winning musician who has shared the stage with legends like James Brown and B. B. King. But I can see in his dark, soulful eyes and kind smile that he will be my friend.

Although I struggle to relate to girls my age, I find consolation in friendships with old souls. Fortunately, my mom can see the places I need to be to make those connections. She never shames me for being different or asks me to change. She watches me carefully and creates a way for me to walk a path of my own.

THIS SUMMER I am fifteen, and my family moves to Austin, Texas. The night before school starts my sophomore year, we are invited to a welcome party at my neighbor's house.

My older brother, Luke, is in the pool with his friend from his new basketball team. They convince me to play "Sharks and Minnows," a game of tag in the pool. They are the sharks. I am the minnow.

My mission is to make it to the other side of the pool without getting caught. I am nervous as they move closer to the edge of the pool where I am waiting to plunge in.

Without thinking, I try to dive over them. I dive too deeply and crash forehead first into the bottom of the pool. My head snaps back, and my chin hits the concrete. I am stunned.

I float limply to the surface as blood clouds the water. The front of my head is split open and my face badly scraped. I cover my forehead with my hands as the boys lift me out of the pool. When I ask to see a mirror, my mom distracts me because she doesn't want me to see my face.

Resting in the hospital, after the surgeon sews up my forehead, I am disoriented but trust I will recover soon. After a few days at home, I realize I am getting worse. I lose parts of myself: my ability to concentrate, my fine motor skills, and my joy. My mind falls into confusion.

During another trip to the emergency room, the doctors tell my mom I have delayed swelling in my brain. On my first day back in my new school, the fluorescent lights, the sound of lockers slamming and students talking loudly, overwhelm me. Everything is amplified.

It feels like a violent invasion of my senses. Trying to process numbers or make simple decisions makes me cry. Even after improving in the following weeks, trying to read one page of a book exhausts me. I still have visible wounds, and the brash high school boys don't hesitate to remind me. "What's wrong with your face?" they mock.

AFTER ONE WEEK in school, it is clear I will not be able to keep up. My mom takes me to the neurologist to be evaluated. When I walk into his office, he says, "I don't see people who have been through what you have been through walk into my office. They are either paralyzed or dead." He explains that the combination of my brain injury along with the way my head snapped back could have resulted in paralysis or death.

"You're lucky," he says cheerfully. I stare at him without responding. I don't feel lucky. I feel like I entered an eerie dream where nothing is real. The changes in my sensory perception are severe and rapid.

I take down all the pictures from my bedroom walls, because I can't stand the visual stimulation. I need to stare at blank spaces. I crave solitude. Listening to people speak feels surreal and exhausting.

I spend most of the day in bed, but no matter how much I sleep, I struggle with severe fatigue. When I look in the mirror, I sometimes think, "Who is that?"

The first poem I write after my accident is called "Trapped":

Trapped in a room of broken ladders
I'm scratching at the door
I throw myself against it
But I'm thrown back all the more

Rising waters drown me
In suffocating grief
My mind clouded in a mist
Of confusion, disbelief

The relentless clock keeps dancing
As helplessly I stand still
Captive in callous darkness
Held against my will.

Depression defines my life. It moves in with such vicious force it becomes difficult to remember a time when it was not with me. My ability to dance is stripped away. Jumps and turns make me nauseated and dizzy.

My ability to concentrate in school dissolves. I am living in a new town, with no friends, stumbling around in the darkness of my own mind. Disoriented and distant when people speak to me, I forget to respond to their questions.

I avoid people as much as possible. It becomes excruciating to occasionally interact with cashiers at coffee shops. "Do not talk to me," I yell inside my head. "Do not ask me about my life. Give me the damn coffee."

To help me rebuild my cognitive endurance, I go to therapy with a man I call Bug Face. Bug Face has a hideous toupee and a fondness for pugs. He has hung framed pug pictures all around his office.

I go to his dimly lit office several days a week and stare at a computer with flashing numbers for hours. It is irritating as hell. I hate every vile number. My job is to respond to the numbers in different ways. This is supposed to help me heal.

Bug Face wants me to solve problems and work on tiny puzzles. I don't want to solve problems. I want to go home, so I can write a new poem and take a nap with my tiny white dog, Josephine.

I find this man repulsive: his blank eyes and condescending tone. After working together for months, he buys me strawberries and cream from a French restaurant and asks me if he can take me to the opera sometime. I say nothing, but tell my mom what happened.

"I think Bug Face just asked me out on a date."

"Gross. You don't have to go back and see him anymore," she says.

"Good," I reply.

FORTUNATELY, I HAVE Shelly. She is my kind hippie teacher who comes to my house to give me short lessons during my recovery, so I don't fall too far behind in school. She works with all the homebound students in our area and is my education angel wearing flowery blouses. I would not make it without her help.

Shelly has a luminous smile and nervous laugh. I stop listening as soon as she starts talking about math, go into a trance, and stare at the way the sunlight falls on her golden-brown hair. Or study the creases in her tan skin, the beautiful lines around her eyes. Our brief sessions exhaust me, but they keep me connected to school and give me a sense that one day I will return.

Along with the changes in my cognitive abilities and mood come changes in my personality. I become less expressive, less interested in life. I start to wake up each day feeling worthless, convinced the world would be a better place if I were dead.

I believe there is some kind of evil inside of me and I need to protect others from this darkness. I hide from my family and begin to contemplate suicide. I want to fall asleep and never wake up. Imagining the end of my life gives me some serenity.

Previously, I had taken advanced classes. Now I am labeled as having a disability. School no longer makes sense to me. I had planned on going to college since I was a little girl, but now I don't know if I will even be able to complete high school.

I retreat into writing poetry. It is all I have left. Writing sustains me and gives me the strength to bear witness to my life. In my notebooks, I take everything I cannot control to the page, so I can shape, sculpt, and redefine through my own vision what it will all mean.

I decide, pen to page, that I am far more than my injuries. I don't know the way out, but I am determined to find it. Nestled in bed with my journal, I pray every day for God to take away the despair.

My pain has a message for me, a message I am not yet ready to hear. It carries the truth of my past: too devastating to embrace yet impossible to forget. God is not abandoning me but allowing me to see where I still need healing.

I want relief from the pain before I look at the true root of my suffering. I want a miracle without confronting where I first felt cut off from love.

The blow to my brain births a painful awakening, a violent rupture and raw call to remember my truth. It forces me to descend into the hidden places within, the places that hold my deepest wounds and greatest power.

THE INJURY SO intensely disrupts my state of consciousness, the past becomes more and more present. The barriers of dissociation start to crack and crumble. The world around me suddenly feels full of pointless, hollow routines and social expectations that no longer make sense to me. I barely recognize myself. A numinous darkness floods into my poetry.

I am living in a disturbing and irresistible dance with my unconscious mind. It bleeds into my sleeping and waking dreams. My inner visions become more vivid and electrifying. I feel haunted and trapped by the ghosts of my interior world.

When I confide in my mom about the depth of my depression, she takes me to see a family counselor. He is balding and wears glasses over his kind brown eyes. His eyes make me feel safe. Though compassionate, the therapist doesn't know how to help me.

He can't understand why I feel helpless and struggle to stay on this earth. He encourages me, but can't see the root of my suffering. I don't talk about my childhood, and he never asks about what I experienced as a little girl.

During many of our sessions, I stare at his bookcases for titles that interest me. One afternoon, as he observes me staring again, he recommends the book *Love's Executioner*, by Dr. Yalom. Through this book, I learn that the Latin root of the word *decide* means "to cut off."

Despite my struggles with depression, I decide to cut myself off from the option of suicide. I know I have to find another way. Our conversations do not set me free from my pain, but they remind me I have a choice: *I can create or I can destroy*.

In another session, he leans forward and says, "When I look at you, I see in one hand you are holding a poem you have written, and in the other hand you are holding a match ready to set it on fire."

He is right. I am at war within myself. There is an artist inside of me. There is also a destroyer. The artist is creative and resilient. But the destroyer is relentless, always searching for a way to silence me. The artist is my original essence. The destroyer is the echo of the man who raped and sold me. His voice has been with me for so long, it has become a part of me.

My mind replays the track: "worthless, worthless, worthless." I am not ready to confess to my counselor about my past, but my abuser's shadow continues to appear in my poetry and songs. I am always circling him—a dance of remembrance and forgetting.

I CONTINUE TO PRAY for a healing miracle. But it does not come the way I want. I want God to grant me immediate relief from my suffering. Instead, the miracle comes through my own voice and the voices of women who faced gender violence and misogyny before me.

Through their books, I see I am not alone. They give me language for the oppression I endured and the courage to continue as a writer. I find bell hooks, Audre Lorde, Adrienne Rich, and Gloria Steinem at our independent bookstores.

Whenever I need comfort, I visit Book People or Book Woman and spend hours discovering new treasures. Even the texture of the paper under my skin soothes me. Feminist theory gives me a meaningful way to process and interpret what happened to me. It helps me feel more grounded, clear, and sane.

Women's voices, women's stories, nourish me when I am hungry for solace and wisdom. "Your silence will not protect you," Audre Lorde reminds me, as I sit on the floor, in a trance, soaking up wisdom between the shelves. I imagine the bookstore is my apothecary.

Each book holds a secret remedy, a key for unlocking silences.

My new guides are more than authors. They are healers. They teach me how all oppressions intersect, how my experience of violence is a part of a broader story of systemic injustice. How my voice is part of a legacy of resistance.

I discover why I felt silenced for so long. I also learn about the privileges I have access to that are not available to other survivors based on a whole spectrum of inequality. This does not diminish the significance of my own trauma, but it gives me a context for that struggle.

In my junior year of high school, I write my first short story for an English class. I portray a young woman who is trying to escape her abusive pimp and entitle it "Maya's Mirror." I describe how Maya covers her bruises with makeup and hides her natural hair under a blonde wig, so she can look like the girls in beauty magazines.

She feels trapped and lonely in a life she did not choose. After a spiritual experience in a breathtaking cathedral, she finds the courage to flee her abuser. The story closes with Maya, finally free, riding a bus out of town.

No one knows Maya is a part of me. I turn the story in to my teacher, whom we call Mrs. G. She is a warm, wise educator with empathetic blue eyes who turns me on to Marge Piercy's poetry and lets me borrow her books.

Covertly, she submits my story to a contest called the Young Texas Writer's Awards, and I win first prize. When she tells me, I am astonished. I never imagined my work would be recognized in this way. I only know writing is helping me stay alive.

I am invited to go to the awards ceremony at the governor's mansion with my parents. When I walk inside to join the reception, decked out in my new black cocktail dress and heels, I hear one of the contest judges saying, "Where's my Maya? Where's my Maya?"

Passionate about the story, he wants to meet "Maya." I am being honored for a story about sex trafficking, but no one asks me what inspired me to write it. If they do ask, I probably will say what I always say when someone asks about the themes of violence in my poetry and songs. "I am passionate about social justice." My response is true but incomplete. Fiction gives me permission to both reveal myself and remain hidden. It allows me to dwell in the dual consciousness of remembrance and forgetting.

"Maya's Mirror" is my first published piece and the first time I receive recognition for my work. This inspires me to share more.

I TELL MY MOM I am ready to publish my first collection of poetry. She takes me to the neighborhood copy shop to make my chapbook.

I carry all my poems in my black messenger bag along with black-and-white photos of my grandmother when she was a child. I choose these vintage images as the artwork for the collection.

My mom introduces me to the customer service lady and tells her about my project. I stare at the floor. I feel exposed and ashamed. I hadn't realized I would actually have to let anyone see my poems, even the copy clerk. I clutch my bag to my chest and won't give it to her.

"If I could just take it for a moment...," she says politely.

I stare at her without moving.

Mom notices I am not responding. "If I could just take a look...," the copy lady repeats. I am resolute. This woman *is not* going to read my poems.

"I think we might need to come back later," Mom offers.

I start walking toward the door, still tightly gripping my bag. We ride home in silence.

A week later, we try again. I move through my fear of being exposed and finally hold a slender volume with a light blue cover and black binding. It is called *defectors from eden*.

After writing poetry for many years and sharing my work at occasional open mics, I start performing at Ruta Maya, a funky coffee shop in the heart of downtown Austin. Here, I begin learning how to trust my voice.

When I am onstage, reading my poetry to strangers and a few poet friends, I sense a force of life within me. I reconnect with my innate power. As I perform the words and sing, I am calling back my soul.

This space becomes another haven for me: the bare concrete floors, vaulted industrial ceilings, vast works of art with Mayan imagery, the smell of fresh coffee beans from Chiapas being roasted and ground, bearded homeless men wandering in, students playing chess and flirting by the smoke shop.

No matter what I want to write, I can share it at the weekly open mic and be heard. This gives me back pieces of my dignity. I expose my inner world, and they listen. It signals a powerful shift in the reclamation of my voice:

"Yes, it is a rising," I say
"A shaking boulder symphony
of a crooked infinity
looking herself in the face
for the very first time
in this flesh-like slate of space"

"But what is that terrible noise,"
he says, covering his ear with one palm
his eye with the other
"That? That?" I say
"Is the throwing off of coffins
and corsets and petticoats
knit of sad secrets
from some fine constitution ..."

"That," I say, "is the end of your echo
in my sweet silver cup
where nameless poets now answer
with a long-forgotten flood
They never had a room

or a breath or a pen
to speak against the silence
they were forced to wear like skin

"And now I tell you plainly
My blood is not for drinking
My voice is not for sinking
and did I forget to mention
I have, also, started thinking."

Now he does not want to stay
He knows I refuse to play
that music of his history
and the romance of a nothing game
In the cement of a man-made day
Only my resurrection will wash the shame away.

The night is not mine to proudly possess
There is fear in the sandpaper black
With the holes you punched out
for stars with your fists
through the silk sky of my back.

Your thoughts on beauty
may feel like a puncture wound
and the darkness may always remain
But I know that I am stronger now
and I will never fear myself again.

The pain is not my enemy. It is just the messenger, but I want to silence the messenger. I wish I could say I found relief. But I can't. It does not come all at once. What I find instead is the power of sacred moments. Moments that help me remember there is beauty worth celebrating even when I am hurting.

After my brain injury, I often focus on what I have lost: my cognitive abilities, education, ballet, energy, and overall sense of clarity. Yet in the stripping away of all these elements, I discover what is essential to me.

I cannot perform or excel in school. I have few friends in my new hometown. But I eventually learn to create my own sacred moments. The miracle does not arrive in immediate release from suffering. It arrives in the form of small, inspired steps.

I write poetry and prayers each day. I travel with my mom to Bonaire, an island just north of Venezuela, and go diving for the first time in a wonderland of breathtaking coral reefs and neon-colored fish. I cuddle up with Josephine, my puppy. I listen to soulful music and dance in my room.

I share my poetry, write lyrics, and sing. When I return to school after a year at home, I perform in plays, where I am usually cast as a villain or seductress, and cofound a creative writing group for students.

My friend Kaiya, who dyes her hair a new color every month, is in charge of advertising our events during the morning school announcements. For one announcement she purrs, "Come to our writers group. It's like *butter*." For Kaiya, this is highest praise, since other than skate shops and tattooed boys, she feels butter is the best life can offer.

She eats butter sticks like candy bars yet stays impossibly thin. She is an irresistible, manic pixie girl with elfish blue eyes and the magical power to lure me out of my hiding place.

Kaiya and I host regular meetings on campus and at Flipnotics, our coffee shop and vintage clothing store, where we set aside time to write together and share our work. It is a place where shy kids can shine. I do not have the community I crave, so we create it together. I begin to come into my voice as a poet and help nurture other young writers.

One December afternoon, I come home from school, and my brother Luke surprises me with an extravagant gift: a beautiful acoustic guitar, so I can start writing my own songs. He has saved his entire college basketball stipend to buy it. Luke tells me he loves my voice and I should learn how to set my poetry to music. He teaches me a few chords, and I start writing my own songs.

Many of my days are filled with pain, but these sacred moments sustain me. I find community among artists, actors, writers, and musicians. If I hadn't experienced my brain injury, I would travel a very different path. My life would be focused on my studies and dance, with little space to experiment, create, travel, and discover what my soul craves. It is not a gentle path of discovery, but it is mine.

Sacred moments do not free me from the unresolved trauma I carry, my original experience of abuse, or the impact of my head injury. What they give me is a way of navigating difficult terrain with some sense of dignity and grace.

As in, I may *feel* like suicide would be the best option right now, *but* I have to swim in the ocean, write a new poem, snuggle with my dog, share my work at a reading, have a coffee date with my mom, go hear a blues show, buy roses.

Live.

chapter four

A Soundtrack for Survival

*When I rose to my resurrection feet
And the dervish of the dead hit the floor
The woman became a warrior
And the poem became a sword.*

As a young artist, I live for moments of grace, and grace finds me through poetry and music. I've never had voice lessons. I don't view myself as a musician.

I only know this fire in my blood, craving release, a fire that will reduce me to ash if I do not honor the call to sing. Whether I am good enough or worthy enough to perform professionally is irrelevant because I feel called. This fire inside of me is far more powerful than my fear.

I devote myself to the process of creation. I learn to channel the pain, untapped power, and wild beauty inside of me into an offering. My art does not have to be perfect. It does not have to be praised. It is my soul medicine because it is my truth.

At eighteen I start singing in downtown Austin. I love Speakeasy, a club with shiny brass railings, a dark wood bar, and red velvet cushions. As I step through an entrance hidden in the alley, I feel transported to the thirties. I become a jazz singer in an old cabaret.

Wearing a sleek black dress, crowned with the spotlight, my life can be whatever I imagine it to be. The music gives me a reason to keep surviving. I perform songs I cowrite with my brothers, who are both prolific songwriters and musicians.

One afternoon, in a furious outpouring, I write the blues melody and lyrics to "Paper Doll":

> *Am I evil? Am I loose?*
> *Am I tight or obtuse?*
> *Will you pin me to the wall*
> *or cut me out, your paper doll?*
>
> *Could you dare*
> *Could you dwell*
> *in an oval of grey*
> *when I refuse to let you*
> *corner me this way?*
>
> *I'll let you fall*
> *I'll let you doubt*
> *I'll let you sweat this one out*
>
> *Don't tell me what is pretty*
> *I just need to know I'm free*
> *from this quest for corsets*
> *that has shaped humanity*

Are we deity? Are we damned
in this promised land
where you hurry to define me
and sculpt me with your hands?

The roots of history have their names
and many men staked a claim
on the wombs and mountains, Mister
Now will you try the same?

My instinct to liberate myself from toxic paradigms surfaces in my lyrics. This process is not intentional. It is primal. I move into the dance of self-definition, observing the gender scripts I inherited, the ones violently played out on my body, and start crafting my way out.

I begin recording "Paper Doll" as the title track to my first album. Stephen Bruton produces it. He is a veteran guitar player who toured with Bonnie Raitt and Bob Dylan. When he hears a few of my demo songs through my friend, blues musician Johnny Nicholas, he invites me to join him in the studio.

I have no music training, except for some piano lessons as a child and less than a year of experience performing in clubs. But Stephen believes in my music, so I take the risk.

I show up at the studio, surrounded by seasoned musicians, trying to describe my vision. I explain what I want through images, colors, and clips of music I love. "Listen to the tone of that bass. The level of distortion. Listen to those drums," I say.

I bring Stephen a list of what I call "touchstones," a guide to help him achieve the sound in my head. I am not trained in the language of music. I only know instinct.

He humors me, but clearly has no idea what to do with me. Right after the record is released, I hear one of my songs, "Pretty Girls Should," on the radio for the first time. It is a meditation on childhood sexual abuse that includes the voice of the perpetrator in the chorus:

Sleep little baby, don't say a word.
Daddy just shot your mockingbird.
Sleep little baby, don't say a word.
Someday you'll bleed like pretty girls should.

I have a song playing on a major radio station about the sexual violation of a child and the shame she experiences, but no one knows the truth. For my record release party, I open at La Zona Rosa for English pop star Dido. A television station interviews me about my work.

I don't feel like a singer. I don't feel I deserve to be there. Yet I know my soul needs to sing. After the show, a woman approaches me and confesses, "I am a survivor of sexual abuse, and your song spoke to me. Thank you."

"Thank you for coming. Thank you for sharing that with me," I say. She is the first survivor of sexual abuse to reach out to me after a performance. I want to bring healing through my voice, but these moments of grace are not enough to heal my own suffering. I try to give others what I have not yet found for myself. I do not know how to make peace with my past.

On another night at La Zona Rosa, I buy paper and art supplies for the audience and tell them I would love for them to write and draw during my performance. They gather around small tables;

some sprawl out on the floor, surrounded by colored pencils and markers. They write confessions, prayers, and quotes and draw images. Afterward, more than fifty people give me their messages and art. In spite of all the pain I carry, it gives me such joy to feel we are creating as a community.

Art does not take away my suffering, but it creates a space to express my full humanity, the grit and raw beauty of my life. I can sing through my wounds. I do not have to force my life into some kind of artificial resolution or cohesion. It can be a complex, evolving, intricate symphony.

My MOM IS the only person I am honest with about my desire to die. When I want to harm myself, I choose not to because I know it would devastate her. For years, she has suggested I take medication for depression, but I resist, fearing I would become someone else if I took a drug.

I do not want to lose myself in a pill. I want supernatural healing.

She keeps saying, "If you had diabetes, you would take medication for diabetes. This is the same thing."

"I don't want to depend on a drug," I say.

I believe the root of my despair is spiritual, but I don't know how to set myself free. I am struggling so often with suicidal thoughts, though, she finally convinces me to see a psychiatrist, who prescribes an antidepressant.

It does not take away the despair, but it takes the edge off. There are whole days when I do not want to kill myself. I intuitively understand it is a temporary fix, a small net catching me from falling deeper into an endless cavern of memories.

The vortex of the past keeps pulling on me, and I need to interrupt the violent force of the descent.

I focus on my music and start dating. I meet my first serious boyfriend in the winter. Zane is wearing a gray fedora and hot pink earmuffs. He immediately attracts my attention as he sets up the stage for a modern dance performance that will take place around the springs. I love his black hair and blue eyes.

After flirting with me for a while, Zane walks away. I am getting ready to leave after my swim when I decide to find him and give him my number.

"I came back to give you my number because I know you would be devastated if you never saw me again," I say, smirking.

With a straight face Zane snaps back, "Well, it's a good thing because I just bought a brand-new pack of razors," insinuating he would have to promptly off himself out of sheer despair in my absence.

I love his dark humor.

He takes his earmuffs off and places them on my head. "Here. Take these, so you have to see me again."

For our first date, Zane takes me to a lavish performing arts space in West Austin. He has a key to get in after hours since he worked there. Zane shows me all the rooms and backstage passageways. When we reach one of the balconies, he passionately pushes me against a column and places his mouth on mine.

I am quickly seduced into his world of theater. I crave him. We have sex, often, in empty theater sets. We speak the same language, the language of art.

Zane's mind is fractured, but brilliant. He is charismatic and moody as hell. One moment ecstatic and the next sullen and withdrawn. When I hear how brutally his dad beat him as a child, I am moved to compassion and become fiercely loyal.

One day he says flatly, "Before I met you, I was in a mental hospital for trying to stab my father."

"What happened?" I ask gently.

"He woke up when I was standing over his bed with a knife in my hand. So they locked me up."

Zane's confession does not frighten me. It only deepens my love for him. I understand. I know what it is like to be brutally hurt and feel there is no way out.

Over time, I witness his anger surfacing, and he begins to direct it toward me. Riding beside him in the car one afternoon, I gently place my hand on the back of his neck.

"If you ever do that again, I will hit you," he growls coldly.

I put my hand back in my lap and do not respond. I understand this is probably a trigger for him, something related to his father. The more I try to help him, the more I see I cannot heal his pain. After a year together, I finally decide to leave.

I struggle in my relationships with men. I am attracted to artists, addicts, the brokenhearted ones with histories of mental illness and abuse. Some of them are kind to me, but our romances don't last very long.

I date a sexy singer-songwriter with large blue eyes and long blond hair who reminds me of Kurt Cobain. He wears a black leather jacket and rides a motorcycle. When we first meet, he stares into my eyes and says dramatically, "I want to kiss your ankle."

"Okay," I say, acting as if it is perfectly ordinary for him to drop to the floor in a crowded club and kiss my ankle.

At one of his shows, he stops in the middle of the set, walks down the stage steps, and brings me a bowl of fresh strawberries to eat while I watch his performance because he knows they are my favorite fruit.

"Here. I know you love strawberries," he says. "I made my friend eat all the bad ones."

"Thank you," I respond, as the whole crowd turns to see why he suddenly left the stage to bring a teenage girl a bowl.

"What was that about?" asks a fan sitting behind me.

"He knows I like strawberries," I say.

We go for rides around Austin on his motorcycle and one night end up on the top of a building downtown admiring the full moon.

"Let's howl at the moon," he says.

I howl as loudly as I can, and he joins me.

I ALSO HAVE MALE friends who crash at my place after their benders. One of them, Sam, a wild-eyed guitar player in his thirties, comes over in a haze of booze and cocaine and then sleeps it off for a couple of days, chain-smoking on the balcony and drinking my coffee. He entertains me with his ridiculous stories, so I let him stick around.

When I am nineteen, Sam takes me backstage at Antone's and introduces me to Billy Gibbons from ZZ Top. All the younger musicians are swarming around Billy, trying to get his attention.

"It looks like everyone wants a piece of you," I observe.

Billy leans over to me and says dryly, "Will you be my bodyguard?"

"Yes," I say, smiling, and place myself between him and the aspiring rockers.

We stand side by side in silence, staring at the stage and quietly listening to the music for the rest of the show.

Sam leans in. "You don't look impressed. Normally, girls are impressed."

"No, I am not impressed," I say.

"I am *trying* to impress you," he complains.

Occasionally, Sam tries to convince me he is an amazing lover and I should *definitely* sleep with him. "Girl, you don't *even* know. You don't even know," he says.

I always decline. After he awkwardly tackles me while we are watching a movie, I tell him, "This is not happening." He gets up to leave and pauses in my doorway, saying defiantly, "I am a *fucking* flower and no one knows." Sam wants to make sure I understand he is a very special, albeit strung out, rock 'n' roll flower before walking out.

He eventually accepts I am not going to fall for him, his introductions to rock stars, or tales of his sexual prowess, so our peculiar friendship continues. I spend time with him because he is eccentric, unhinged, and highly entertaining. In his sober moments, we have soul talks, trade poetry, and listen to trip hop at his place.

Most of all, Sam makes me laugh, and I need to laugh. One night when we are listening to records, he says, "Girl, you're drugs. You're *drugs.*" I grin, knowing this is the greatest compliment he can give.

He continues, "You're like a treasure I found when I was walking on the beach and I put it in my pocket and I want to hide it in my basement, so no one else can see it."

I try to talk him into going to rehab, but he isn't interested, so I slowly start to distance myself. Sam is never going to be someone I can trust. I have always been the confidante, the caretaker. I need someone who can take care of me, too.

*W*HEN I MEET Rosalyn Rosen through my music manager, Kevin, I am starved for connection, a real soul companion. She immediately recognizes me for the mystic-old-soul-poet I am and embraces me with compassion. Although I am thirty years younger than she is, we know from our first meeting we are kindred spirits. I begin to feel less alone.

As a playwright and filmmaker, Rosalyn spends weeks in solitude focused on her work, but she often sends me passionate, insightful notes to remind me she is with me. She encourages me to read all the diaries of Anaïs Nin and the work of therapist Alice Miller.

When we meet for coffee or relax with a glass of wine at her place, we talk about Jewish mysticism, Buddhist philosophy, poetry, film, music, and healing trauma. She shares stories about her parents surviving the Holocaust and how it shaped her writing.

Rosalyn devotes herself to inner healing and cultural healing through the arts, and she is what Alice Miller calls an "enlightened witness," someone who can bear witness to suffering with compassion. I print every email she sends me and tape them into my journal between poems, prayers, drawings, and photographs. Her notes are little love letters filled with spiritual wisdom. Each word is sacred to me.

In the mornings, I make coffee, light a candle, and listen to the compositions of Eric Satie. I read passages from Anaïs. "Reality doesn't impress me," she writes. "I only believe in intoxication, in ecstasy, and when ordinary life shackles me, I escape, one way or another. No more walls."

Her words give me courage to continue on my own path as a poet and singer. She reminds me to be bold: "If you do not breathe through writing, if you do not cry out in writing, or sing in writing, then don't write, because our culture has no use for it."

In my small apartment with a view of Lady Bird Lake, I write in my journal each day. The space is mostly bare except for the antique steamer trunk filled with my notebooks, a guitar, keyboard, twin mattress on the floor, my stereo, and a faceless black mannequin in the corner. At sunset, I watch thousands of bats swarm in one long stream from the Congress Street Bridge over my balcony, disappearing into the dark.

When I pray, I do not pray for healing anymore. I pray for courage. I come out of hiding to sing in clubs around Austin, then return to my solitude by the water. I speak to my mom, Rosalyn, and the occasional boyfriend. I give my number to only a few people.

If I don't have a show, I can go days at a time without speaking to anyone. At night, I wander the downtown streets alone, observing people, slipping into bars to hear blues or jazz, writing poetry in an Irish pub or crowded café.

I stop to talk with homeless women, and they tell me about the violence they experience on the streets and in the shelters. Mostly, I listen.

Sometimes they ask me to pray for them. I never mention my faith, but they sense they can ask. So, I pray aloud and ask if they want a hug. They always want a hug. Usually, I don't see them again. We are soul sisters passing in the night.

One evening a Native American tarot card reader calls out to me as I am walking down Congress Street. I have never seen her before. She stops me and gazes deeply into my eyes. She says, "My daughter is seven years old, and she is having nightmares. Will you pray for her?"

"Yes. Of course."

While she reads her cards, I sit on a park bench and talk with her little girl for a while. She quietly tells me about the fear that comes to her at night.

"There is darkness in my room."

"Your mom asked me if I would pray for you. Can I pray for you?"

"Yes," she says and closes her eyes.

I pray aloud for her to be blessed, protected, and guided. It seems strange to me that her mom and other women on the street ask me to pray for them, yet somehow completely natural. It is as if our souls are having a conversation that our rational minds cannot understand. When they ask, my soul says yes without comprehending what this could mean.

On another night stroll, I go to the capitol building. It is almost completely empty, but they are still accepting visitors. I take the elevator to the fourth-floor women's restroom. I had previously discovered I might be able to climb out and sit on a ledge on the side of the building.

So I lock the door, open the window, and crawl out onto the stone ledge. I can see the patrol cars circling below, but I am hidden from view. I search my satchel for a pen but find only black eyeliner and lipstick. So I write a poem with makeup, as the moonlight drenches my journal page and gray pigeons circle around me.

I feel most alive on the edge.

During my downtown walks, I often fall into a trance, searching for parts of my soul, for something I cannot name. When I meet someone on the street I connect with, I listen. While becoming a compassionate witness for others, I am learning how to become a compassionate witness for myself.

When I come home alone, I dance around in my black lingerie, surrounded by candlelight. I am taking the pills the psychiatrist gave me, but I still feel haunted.

I play with this haunting in surreal photo shoots with different photographers. In one shoot, I set up a communion scene on an elaborate tomb in the MLK graveyard. I bring a loaf of fresh bread, wine, and a chalice. While I enact this ritual, an affirmation of life in the presence of death, a monarch butterfly lands on my arm and stays there, resting.

I also experiment with other elements of religious myths and Christian iconography. I borrow a snake to hold and bring a red apple to stab and bite. We visit St. Mary's Cathedral, where I kneel at the altar and pretend to drink holy water. At the end of the shoot, I am posing by a gate, and a nun comes up, places her hand gently on my shoulder, and says, "You are blessed."

"Thank you, Sister."

Then she turns and walks away.

Some might consider my experiments sacrilegious. But for me, they are holy. I am dancing with my ghosts and reclaiming symbols that caused me pain and confusion. I am disrupting the religious abuse of my childhood by subverting the old meanings and placing symbols in a new landscape of creative play.

As A PERFORMER, I receive conflicting messages from others about who I am. Some members of the audience tell me they feel a sense of peace when they hear me sing. One friend shares, "I walk into the club feeling burdened, but when I listen to your music I feel relieved, like a weight has been lifted from me."

Some friends call me an angel and healer. Others who encounter my work tell me I am "too dark" or "too sexual." I meet women who want me to pray for them. Yet I am also cornered by multiple people claiming they want to cast demons out of me. Yes, demons.

A middle-aged lady with short curly brown hair and glasses rushes up to me after a show, firmly plants her palm right on my forehead without asking, and says, "I want to pray for you." Then she starts speaking in tongues and telling the devil to leave.

Some people in my parents' church community say I am prophetic. Others claim I am "too seductive." These severely conflicting responses hurt and confuse me.

I know I have a loving heart and relentless commitment to being a healing presence in the world. Yet sometimes there does not seem to be enough space for my full humanity in what some call "the light." If their light denies my truth, my pain, my rage, my body as a woman, my sexuality, it is not the untamed grace I crave, a grace expansive enough to hold all of me, undivided, without shame.

The more I share the truth of my experience, the more I am labeled as "dark." Yet the homeless women, the sexual assault survivors at my shows, the artist friends I love and encourage view me with a radically different perspective. To them, I am a soul sister they can trust with their deepest pain.

I can see that what some refer to as darkness is not "evil," but the realm of mystery, the realm of the unknown. The word *dark* is pointing to all that is hidden, rejected, buried, silenced, and disowned.

For those who are honest about their own suffering, struggles, and human desires, I am not a threat or a trigger. But for those who cannot bear to accept their own shadows, their own sexuality, their own silenced parts, I awaken their core wound, and they blame me for this.

I leave the local church because I know I will not come to wholeness there. I leave to heal myself. I will not abandon my connection with God. I know it will only deepen with my departure. I am called to a new chapter in my Divine love story, where I do not have to leave any part of myself behind.

*M*Y MANAGER BOOKS a gig for me to open for Terry Bozzio, the brilliant drummer who played with rock legend Frank Zappa. I feel at home on the stage, channeling my voice from the center of the earth. When I sing, I taste freedom.

Still riding the rush of the show, the club owner comes over to pay me. "You remind me of a female Jim Morrison," he says.

I feel he can recognize this strange path I am traveling. "Thanks," I say, taking the cash and feeling a little less crazy.

Maybe there is a place for me here.

After my set, I watch Terry play. His music mesmerizes me. He moves like a fluid dancer around his enormous drum set, percussion instruments he collected from his travels around the world. I am ecstatic to have opened for such a powerful artist, but I question how long I will be able to sustain this. I know I am on the edge of collapse.

I record songs with producer Mitch Watkins, who toured for years as Leonard Cohen's guitar player. One day in his studio, I express my self-doubt. "I don't really know what I am doing," I say as we listen to a track. "I just go on instinct."

He looks at me thoughtfully. "Trust yourself, Brooke. You know *exactly* what you are doing. Don't let anyone tell you differently."

I also work with my friends Charlie Sexton and David Boyle, who played keys on my first record. They encourage me as a singer and poet, but I am barely surviving. I know it will not last.

*T*HE WALLS I built to protect myself in childhood continue to crumble. The nightmares increase, and more flashbacks flood in. I can no longer look away. Scenes of my abuse surround me everywhere I go. Sitting in a café with my mom, trying to hold a conversation, I see my perpetrators encircling me, as if they are ghosts.

There is no escape. Helping others, my music, prayer, the night walks, the solace of Rosalyn's friendship, and my mom's love are vital and lifesaving. But these graces are not enough to make the ghosts go away. I start to feel I am seven years old again, trapped, terrified, and ashamed.

In one moment, my chest feels as though it is caving in. I struggle to breathe. In the next, I am numb, lost in a trance. I stay in bed for most of the day now. I write prayers and poems in my journal and try to avoid my family.

I drive around town listening to music without a destination and become angry when anyone asks where I have been. I scream with PJ Harvey, "You're not rid of me. I'll make you lick my injuries." And cry out with Ani DiFranco, "I am not a pretty girl. That is not what I do."

They give me permission to channel this deep rage I cannot yet call my own. I listen to many artists, from Radiohead to Portishead, Jeff Buckley to Björk, but it is this primal female rage that calls to me.

I don't feel angry in my own life. I feel despair. But their voices give me permission to reclaim the part of me who wants to yell, "No more!"

I SHARE ALMOST EVERYTHING with my mom except for the truth of what happened to me when she was in the hospital. She knows I am struggling, each day fighting for my life, but she doesn't know the source of my suffering.

The memories consume me. They are no longer recollections or passing apparitions. The violence surrounds me on every side. I am descending into the underworld, deeper and deeper into a cavern without end.

The deeper I fall, the more brutal the imagery. He is there with me. The man I most fear, the man who trained me to wage war against myself. I know I must confess. My body will not let me forget. I see no other way out.

Finally, when the pain of my flashbacks becomes unbearable, I tell my parents I need to speak with them. We meet in their living room, and I finally share what I have always known, what I could not bear to know.

"The nanny. He raped me. He gave me to other men."

I don't share many details. Just what I need them to know. As I speak, I see him standing over the body of that lost little girl who could not bear to know the truth.

I offer my voice for her. Tears stream down my face. My parents cry with me, stunned and devastated. My mom sobs as she holds me, repeating, "I am so sorry. I am so sorry." My dad, in tears, echoes her, "I am so sorry I wasn't there for you." I cannot stay with them and witness their grief. I don't want to keep talking, so I return to their guest room to be alone.

The next morning at the kitchen table, it is obvious the pain is consuming my parents. This is one of the reasons I did not want to tell them.

My dad growls, "I want to find him and kill him."

"That won't help me heal. I don't want you to end up in jail. I need you here," I plead.

He tries to calm down and to focus on how he can help me. I know I won't experience the justice my dad wants.

I was seven when I was abused and have no evidence to help convict my trafficker. I only have my truth, my story, the pain ravaging me. I know that like the vast majority of rapists, my abuser will never spend a day in jail.

If I am to ever experience justice, I will have to create it for myself. Even if my perpetrator spent the rest of his life in prison, it would not set me free from all the pain: my PTSD, my depression, my piercing sense of worthlessness.

His punishment now is irrelevant to my healing. I choose to devote myself to my recovery above all else. This is not about him. If my recovery depends on his suffering, I will never be free. This is my justice: to heal, to thrive, to rise and reclaim my life. Speaking my truth is the beginning of freedom.

*O*VER THE NEXT few weeks, I start collecting photographs of myself as a little girl. I search through boxes in my parents' garage filled with my childhood artwork and stories. I move my materials into the smallest room of their house, a tiny office with enough space for one desk and a blanket on the floor. It becomes my little cave, a place to feel safe and held.

I listen to Tori Amos's live version of "Precious Things" over and over while creating collages and drawing scenes of my abuse. I take childhood photos, tape them into my journal, and use a red pen to cover the face and body of that sweet little girl with all the demeaning names my rapist called me.

"So you can make me cum. That doesn't make you Jesus," I wail along with Tori.

I also write on my own arms and legs with red ink. I am bearing witness. I am covering myself with words, all the unspeakable words. I am purging myself of his poison. I am making the violence visible, so it no longer has power over me.

It is my healing ritual. I am calling back the pieces of my soul, the parts that fled when they violated me. In the evenings, I climb out of the office window onto the roof with a bottle of cabernet and stare at the Hill Country stars.

After a long night of flashbacks throwing me back to when I was assaulted for pornographic films, I write about my experience of trafficking and sing it to myself. One verse says,

Hands bound above my head
On the executioner's bed
The murder was so slow
It's happening all over

It's happening all over me
Can I go home now?
Where's my Daddy?

Then the chorus follows,

I want to know where the little girls go
who never got to give themselves away
How do you say unspeakable things?

My parents give me space to grieve and offer gentle words of encouragement when I want to talk, but they are helpless to take away the pain. When I am not writing or drawing, I rest in bed and stare at the ceiling listening to the Tori Amos record *Boys for Pele*. "I need a big loan from the girl zone," she cries in my ears.

When the last page of my blue journal is filled with drawings, I wrap the cover in a slender piece of black leather and take it to Rosalyn's place.

"This is what happened to me," I say when she opens the door. I hand over the notebook. "Oh, sweetheart," she says and gives me a hug. "I will keep it safe."

THE NEXT TIME I take the stage at Steamboat, my band is already improvising. The drums lure me into a trance, and I dance, slowly swaying in the spotlight. I wear a black camisole and long black skirt with platform heels. Behind me, the vivid abstract paintings of my new artist boyfriend are projected along with lines from my lyrics. Black candelabras with white candles adorn the front of the stage.

I don't begin the planned set. I channel the energy that comes to me, singing a new song of freedom. I am one with the music, and in that moment the music carries all the wisdom I need. I can see faces in the crowd, illuminated and expectant.

I pray silently for every person entering the club to find healing and peace. I offer all I am, all that is left of me. I follow this with Rosalyn's favorite song, repeating the chorus, *"I am still here and holy breathing."*

I open my soul to the path of recovery and perform a poem to take me back to what I know: my voice, my truth. It is my broken-hearted gift and beautiful resistance.

The women here are in need of voice lessons.
Breath-controllers ride & thrust

demeaning the fullness.
Upon us the force is early applied.
We quickly learn the way of silence.

They demand our flesh.
Instruct us to despise our own discernment,
doubt our knowing.
The survivor is forever on trial
warring against the twisting of every sentence.

Electrocution of elocution.
Everywhere is preached
the glamorous disease, vogue virus.

My body, the bodies of all women and girls
are the raw material of production, consumption.
Eroticize the inequality and bank on it, sexy industry.

The message is bull-horning clear
This is who you are.
This is why you are here:
to be pleasing
according to the shifting demands of man
until our only power becomes that of seduction.

For your little girls, what is left?
How my mind is an axe,
my heart a voluptuous cup overflowing,
my soul a holy siren.

What I am cannot be contained
on your magazine page.
What I am cannot be shamed
into submission.

I decline subscription.
You will not win
this one.

chapter five

Mary Magdalene Blues

I am a daughter of the burning.
What I have chosen will not be taken from me.

SINCE THE DARKNESS HAS NOT PASSED, I am learning to see in the dark. Since the pain has not passed, I am learning to sing songs of solace. That is why I love the blues.

The blues takes moments of struggle and loss and transforms them into a communal offering, an affirmation of life. If I can still sing about the pain, sing through the pain, it has not defeated me.

As a nineteen-year-old poet and activist, I join an outreach project to serve incarcerated women. When I visit a jail for the first time, I sing a blues song about Mary Magdalene.

Many of the women were convicted on drug possession and prostitution charges. They do not belong here, in this sterile facility with gray floors and dull fluorescent lights, cut off from the color of the world. For most, they were simply trying to escape the pain of a lifetime of abuse. Through soul talk, sharing food, music, and prayer, we make the jail a sacred space.

This evening, as I perform the Mary Magdalene song, I stand in an outdoor courtyard with dim lights in front of more than a hundred inmates just after sunset. I sing a cappella, with all the power I can channel through my body.

The core message of my song is this: Nothing can separate us from Divine Love. Grace is wild enough, vast enough, to include us all. It heals our shame.

The women in Del Valle jail have been told lies about who they are. They have been silenced. After years of having their boundaries violated, they crossed lines in an effort to medicate the pain or survive.

Some confess they are even scared to leave the jail because of what could happen to them when they do. Will they relapse or be abused again?

I tell them, "No matter what lies you have been told, you can return to the truth of who you are: beloved. Love can liberate us from shame."

My FRIEND IS driving us to a festival in Houston. During the ride we talk about spirituality and the challenges men and women face in creating intimacy, particularly as a result of gender scripts that limit the expression of our full humanity.

We are laughing and enjoying the road trip from Austin when a teenage boy swerves into our lane going eighty miles an hour and hits us head-on. We are going about sixty. His truck then swings around, crashes into our left side, flies back into the air, and lands on the hood of the car behind us.

The car behind us then rear-ends my friend's car. We are hit on three sides at high speeds. The car completely collapses around us.

I am instantly knocked unconscious. The next thing I feel is being cut out of mangled steel by the jaws of life. I am pulled out onto a stretcher and hear a woman speaking to me, but I cannot respond. I am in and out of consciousness as the EMS team rushes me into the helicopter to be flown to Houston Memorial Hospital.

A nurse cuts the clothes off of my body with large scissors. I hear a man groaning in pain and slowly turn my head to the left. Just beside me is a young black man whose face was kicked in by a horse.

My body is covered in bruises. The nurses keep poking me and saying, "Does this hurt? Does this hurt?"

"Yes. Yes," I whisper.

The physician attending the man with the bloody, caved-in face keeps poking him, too, and asking if it hurts. The patient clearly can't respond. He is either in too much pain, in a state of shock, or physically unable to form the words. I feel protective of him, seeing his pain and how callous the doctor is being.

The doctor says, frustrated, "I can't help you if you don't respond." The young man turns his head toward me. Our eyes meet. We share a moment of recognition.

I can see his agony. Half of his face is brutally crushed. His doctor presses again, this time more irritated when his patient does not respond.

"It's not like I *enjoy* this," the doctor finally snaps.

This pisses me off.

"Yes, you do!" I yell across the ER. "You all enjoy this!"

My nurse says, "Be quiet!"

But this lack of compassion is not acceptable to me.

Fortunately, after my outburst, the doctor backs off.

I rest in the hospital for a few days. My foot is shattered. The doctors observe a persistent electrical issue with my heart. They also decide to monitor the aftermath of my brain injury, particularly since I have already experienced one as a teen.

My body is covered in bruises from the impact of the collision and my bones are broken, but I can't take any painkillers because I have allergies to them. So the nurses give me aspirin.

My mom was out of state during the car crash, so it takes a day for her to reach me. When she arrives, she stays by my side and speaks with the doctors to make sure I have everything I need.

"What can I get you?" she asks when I wake up.

"Pen, paper, and a coffee."

She smiles and comes back with everything from the nurses' station. I find comfort in doing what I always do after trauma. I write.

For me, to write is to take back my life, to identify what belongs to me and what I desire to release. Ultimately, I decide what these moments will mean. Moving pen across page is a path back to sovereignty, a choice to create in the midst of loss.

It is my art of resistance. It is how I see in the dark.

In that hospital bed, I write prayers, poems, words of gratitude for small gifts: a black coffee, the sound of my mother's soothing voice, my own breath. When I am too tired to write, I watch black-and-white Hitchcock films and sleep.

After I am released from the hospital, my mom stays with me in a little modern cottage just south of Austin. My blood pressure is dropping so low I struggle to stay upright. I have to use a wheelchair and then a walker to support my foot.

In the haze of pain and confusion, all I envisioned for my life in music slowly starts to fade. My desire to pursue a career as a singer and songwriter suddenly abandons me. It no longer seems important or real.

I do not recover as quickly as I hoped. I go to physical therapy for a year to regain strength and range of motion in my foot. During this time of waiting and allowing my body to heal, I immerse myself in the Song of Solomon. I want to know how to experience myself as one who is unconditionally loved, unconditionally valued, no matter what my circumstances may be.

Whether I am healthy or ill, celebrated for my creative work or not, single or in a relationship, praised for my appearance or ignored, achieving my dreams or struggling to survive, I want to know, in my depths, breath by breath, that nothing can separate me from love.

I want to feel worthy in my very being, even in a state of complete rest, even when I cannot perform or help others. I ask myself, "Who am I without all that gives me a sense of value and identity? Who am I when all this is stripped away?"

This is the severe mercy of trauma and significant loss. It awakens me to what is essential, no matter how painful it may be. The wound is the opening to a new way of seeing, yet it feels like madness before it becomes medicine.

My body is covered with wounds, so my body is covered with eyes, these openings to new sight. For me, the wounds never closed; they kept opening and opening and opening until they became something else entirely. A portal for my soul to move through, shine through, and voice buried truth. One wound became so vast she shape-shifted into a cave I could pass through to the other side, a passage tomb. It is at the winter solstice, the depth of darkness, that the light finally strikes you.

I'VE ADORED GOD since I was a child, whispering prayers in the dark. I felt the presence of Jesus and the angels. Yet I knew something vital was missing.

What was most noticeably missing for me were the voices and stories of women.

I lost my voice for the first time when I was trafficked at seven. I also witnessed my mom physically lose her capacity to speak as a result of her illness. Then, when I was taken to church, a place that was supposed to help people connect with God, I felt there was no place for my truth, the voice of my soul.

After my car accident, I need sacred stories that include me. I am weary of this splitting off and suppression of feminine wisdom. During the hours I can stay awake, I continue to study the Song of Songs.

The first line that stays with me appears in Chapter 1, when the woman who is referred to as both Beloved and Bride describes her family history and trauma she experienced. She confides that her angry brothers forced her to serve in their vineyards. Her family treated her like a servant. "My own vineyard I have neglected," she reveals.

This simple truth pierces through my confusion in the wake of my head injury and confinement to bed. I feel I know her. I feel I *am* her.

As a child and teen, I did not receive the help I needed to heal from the trauma of sex trafficking. I neglected my inner world, my own vineyard, in an effort to survive, seek acceptance, and prove my worth. Yet ultimately, it left me feeling depleted and alone.

This line reverberates in my soul: "My own vineyard I have neglected." I start to explore this question: What would it look like to cultivate my own vineyard? What belongs to me? What has been entrusted to me? How do I want to tend to this?

Throughout the Song, the woman's Lover praises her as sacred, beautiful, and valuable, but it takes her time to trust and receive this love. At times her Lover asks for her to reveal more of her beauty to him, so he can enjoy all of who she is. He calls out to her and tells her that "winter has passed," spring has arrived, and "the season of singing has come."

Although he desires intimacy with her, she is hiding. Perhaps out of fear or the remaining traces of shame she carries from the past. He invites her to come out and allow herself to be fully seen and heard. He cries out, "My dove in the clefts of the rock, in the hiding places on the mountainside, show me your face, *let me hear your voice*."

This passage is my first encounter with Scripture where I see a man call out for a woman to share *her voice*. As weary and defeated as I feel, I know I am also being called to come out of hiding and allow myself to be seen for who I am, to share the voice of my soul without shame or fear.

After a period of time apart, the woman decides to search for her Lover. Until that moment, he has been in pursuit of her. Now she is filled with a fierce desire to be with him.

This starts a cycle of ecstatic intimacy and painful moments of separation that lead to deeper passion. During one of these periods of separation, the Beloved searches for her Lover, but cannot find him. She calls, but he does not answer.

On her quest she is violently attacked by those she refers to as "the watchmen." As these guards make their rounds in the city, they find her alone and abuse her. She says, "They beat me and bruised me; they took away my cloak." Yet she is not deterred in her pursuit of love.

In my own life, I view the violent guards as the men in my past who claimed to know God, yet used and abused me, stripping away my dignity and sense of safety. But just like the woman in the Song, my hunger for the Divine only deepens.

In a later passage, friends of the woman see her coming out of the wilderness, leaning on her Lover. After all her searching, after being treated like a servant and attacked by those who should protect her, she is weary and lets herself be supported.

This is what I want: to be carried out of the harsh wilderness, to be comforted and guided home. Just like the Beloved in the story, I want to be brought back to life with lavish love, emanating from deep within.

In my prayers, I join with her in saying, "Love is as strong as death, its ardor unyielding as the grave. It burns like a blazing fire, like a mighty flame. Many waters cannot quench love; rivers cannot sweep it away."

Although I am not performing in clubs or recording music during this time of healing, I am learning more about the true value of my voice. The value of my voice is not in how I can move an audience or inspire others. It is in how I can reveal the truth of my soul.

My voice is the gold bridge between my interior world and exterior world, the realm of flesh and the realm of spirit, the seen and the unseen, between heaven and earth.

"Let me hear your voice," says Divine Love. "Come out of hiding. I have been waiting."

Whether I am whispering prayers in the dark, singing blues in a jail, or performing onstage, I know my voice has value because I remember my spiritual birthright. I am the Beloved.

As mystic poet Rabia wrote, "I was healed when all I once feared, I could love."

I once feared my own truth. I feared what would happen if my voice was finally heard. Yet it is my voice that saves me and prepares the way for love.

chapter six

House of Lies

We are the women of the water.
We are the keepers of the deep.

AFTER MY CAR ACCIDENT AND A year of recovery through physical therapy, I decide to leave Austin. My desire to be whole has become far more powerful than my fear of suffering.

For years, I wanted only to sing and perform my poetry as a recording artist. Yet my passion to follow a path in music fractured and faded as my broken bones healed.

It no longer makes sense to me. I don't want to entertain a crowd. I want to listen to my own soul voice and find the remedy for this relentless pain. The brutal collision not only shattered my body. It altered my consciousness.

Once again I am stripped naked of my sense of safety and identity. I receive generous offers to work with successful producers and record label interest. Yet my soul recognizes it is time to leave Austin behind and continue my quest for healing.

I don't understand why, but I feel drawn to study creative writing in Boulder, Colorado. I can no longer envision a career in music, but

I know I have to write. My core desire is to grow as a writer, and I need mentorship for the next evolution of my work.

Courting record labels, producers, and audiences no longer matters to me. It is like wading in the shallows when I crave the rush of the deep. The whole culture and climate around music feels hollow and dehumanizing.

I love creating, but I am weary of all the trappings, everything attached to the business of art. I am tired of older men in the industry commenting on my appearance, misunderstanding my lyrics, and treating me like a product to sell. I don't want to have to please and captivate anyone. I want to disappear.

I start my studies at the University of Colorado and then migrate over to Naropa University, a small liberal arts school founded by a Tibetan Buddhist monk. I hear they integrate contemplative practices with their innovative program in poetics. It sounds like the refuge I am seeking.

At an opening ceremony on campus, after a series of Tibetan Buddhist chants, students are given a seed to plant in the earth to represent their intention for their time at Naropa. Holding my seed, I search within for my intention. One word comes to me with clarity and power. *Voice*. Sitting cross-legged on the lawn, I dig a hole past the grass into the black earth and whisper within, *"Voice. Voice. Voice."*

I RENT A SMALL studio over a soul food restaurant and music club in Boulder across the street from the Fox Theater, where most of the touring bands perform. The owner, Andy, also runs a record shop down the street and loves poetry, so he hosts musicians and poets for showcases and open mics. He curates intimate events with singer-songwriters like English crooner Piers Faccini. I can walk down one flight of stairs, open the next door, and enter his world.

Andy is a warm, outspoken, and thoughtful man who looks out for me. When I am at the bar one night sipping a glass of red wine alone, he confides, "I worry about you, Brooke." I laugh and keep writing in my journal.

He studies me carefully. I look up. "I am *fine*." He watches me meet new men at the bar and take them upstairs to my studio. A couple of his employees come up to my apartment on their breaks to drink or snort coke.

"I have daughters your age. You should be more careful," he says. I don't listen, but I appreciate his care.

I share a hallway bathroom with five guys who continuously smoke pot and invite me along on their adventures: parties often involving drum circles, reggae shows, and, most important, a Björk concert at Red Rocks. They are kind, free-spirited, and charming, a perpetually high wolf pack I can easily run with.

At a salsa dance night downtown, I meet a writer from Jordan. Omar is tall and striking, with olive skin, thick black hair, and a sharp button-down shirt. A powerful contrast to most of the men I meet in Boulder who look like they are on their way to see a jam band.

I am immediately infatuated. After our first date, I decline to sleep with him because I want to get to know him a bit better. This confuses him.

"American women only want sex," Omar says confidently.

"Where did you hear that?" I ask.

"I saw it on the TV. But you know they work too much. So when you pull over and ask them, they just want to go home."

As strange as his comment was, I keep seeing Omar because he is sexy, intelligent, and I am curious to learn more about how he views the world. I go over to his place one afternoon, and he shows me photographs of his family.

Omar holds up a photograph of his father in white robes and a turban. "In my country, we have much land and many goats. My father has three wives. Do not be afraid."

"I see."

I am still intrigued. We have conversations about cultural differences, gender roles, religion, film, and art. Unfortunately, after a few dates Omar becomes very possessive and thinks he should start telling me what to do.

He shows up uninvited at my door on Saint Patrick's Day. I plan to go out to some pubs with my friends. When I explain that I already have plans, he says, "I do not want you with those other men. I do not know them."

"You are welcome to come with us," I offer.

"I will not come with you. I will wait for you downtown alone. You will come to my house and have dinner. Then we will have sex. You will spend the night, and in the morning we will have breakfast," he says.

"I am not spending the night," I reply.

Though Omar is extremely handsome, he has quickly moved from intriguing to disturbing. When I tell my buddies about this, they laugh.

"You know, if you don't sleep with a guy by the third date, he will think you are not interested in him," one says.

"What? Who came up with that?" I ask.

"But you should stay away from that guy. He sounds crazy."

"Agreed," I respond.

My love life in Boulder is mostly absurd, not disturbing. There is the bearded mountain man with long brown hair and chiseled features who carries a bowie knife on his handmade leather belt. He lives in a log cabin about an hour from town.

There is the blue-eyed entrepreneur who takes me to bluegrass shows. His entire downtown office is devoted to smoking pot and watching art films.

There is the teacher by day/bouncer by night, a sweet, forgetful drunk. He insists on having me recite poems during sex, which is more amusing than erotic for me. We also read the dictionary while naked in bed because he is turned on by how I read the etymology of words.

There is the slender saxophone player with long black hair and a passion for jazz and Tim Burton movies. After a while, I lose track.

It is a blur of seductions fueled by both my soul wounds and my cravings. A dance of hungers. Although I would love a real relationship, passion integrated with intimacy, I am not yet integrated within myself.

Sex is an escape, a drug, a shortcut to ecstasy. I want love, too, yet I have sex the way I drink: to ease the pain, to feel alive, to ride the rush and forget the past in passing moments of pleasure. Ultimately, it leads me to re-create the suffering I desperately want to escape: this cycle of feeling used and devalued by men.

These sexual experiences are consensual and often filled with intense physical pleasure, but the exchange lacks soul. There is no place for my deeper truth, and it leaves me feeling more alone and hollow. I left all I knew behind, my family, my friends, my music. But I do not find a haven in Boulder.

So, I find solace where I can: in the bodies of men who desire me, but never see me for who I am. My desire for pleasure is sacred, but I am channeling it in a way that leads to despair.

At Naropa University, I take a class called Contemplative Practice and learn ways of cultivating mindfulness through meditation. My gentle, wise African American professor tells us on the first day of class, "I am not interested in converting you to Buddhism. Whatever your spiritual tradition may be, meditation can help you deepen it."

On breaks I visit the café and wait in line for a coffee along with young hippies, punks, poets, and the Tibetan monks who come to visit. The small, quiet campus attracts young seekers, activists, and artists who don't fit into traditional universities.

It is refreshing to hear a spiritual teacher offer tools for growth and understanding rather than requiring we submit to a religious doctrine. My only exposure to religious teachers before this class emphasized the importance of having the right worldview. Failure to accept the teacher's worldview as absolute truth was framed as rebellion. Although I study Tibetan Buddhist philosophy in my class, I am not searching for a new religion, but practices that can lead to liberation.

We meditate in circles, resting on our blue cushions, following our breath. I start to feel greater peace as I learn more about how to befriend my own body and mind. "Notice your thoughts and let them pass without clinging to them or rejecting them. They are like clouds in the sky," he instructs us.

His teachings are powerfully simple and pragmatic. "This is not about belief. This is about your own experience. If a tool is useful, use it. If it doesn't work for you, let it go."

My professor also introduces me to the concept of "fundamental goodness" as it was defined by Naropa founder Trungpa Rinpoche. Fundamental goodness is the innate goodness within each of us. After being told by my abusers and many religious teachers that I was fundamentally bad, mindfulness meditation helps me return to the knowledge of what is good and true in my humanity. In my Contemplative Practice class and readings, I discover a worldview that opens me to the possibility of self-compassion.

Studying Buddhism does not persuade me to become a Buddhist, but it gives me a different frame to view my human experience and the root of my suffering. Meditation creates the space for me to witness the ways I have been subjected to mind control as a child. Through the systematic use of trauma, I was forced to believe the lies of my abusers. I was taught to fear myself and reject my truth.

A simple daily meditation practice empowers me to see through false frameworks. I can distance myself from indoctrination by becoming the witness, a witness to my own thoughts and patterns. I can see internally how their words, symbols, and narratives were constructed and arbitrary. The invisible becomes visible. The unconscious becomes conscious.

Becoming a student of my own consciousness is not a new religious identity. Mindfulness simply helps me bring my attention to what is arising for me breath by breath, in my body. This enables me to discern the passing of thoughts and emotions as separate from my core awareness. Once I tap into this core awareness, my own enlightened witness, I can begin to separate out the stories others forced on me.

I awaken, witness the house of lies within me, and prepare to leave it behind. Through a process of observation, noting my repeating patterns, stories, and echoes from my experiences of trafficking and religious abuse, I intentionally renounce and refuse spiritual agreements that trap me in a cycle of suffering.

I write out the toxic agreements I made at a soul level about who I am and what is possible for me. These include agreements about the nature of God and humanity. The more aware I become of my agreements, the more empowered I am to live by my own truth.

As I learn in my Contemplative Practice class and the writings of Buddhist teachers, we experience pain when we encounter trauma, hurt, or loss in our lives. But we perpetuate suffering by the stories we tell ourselves about what happened. When pain meets healing truth and tender awareness, grief can be released, and we are free to create new meaning.

Over time, the painful events become integrated into our greater life narrative. There is a cleansing and freedom in this process. But often it is the stories we tell about our initial pain that keep us stuck and feed the cycle of suffering.

Mindfulness is not positive thinking. It is far more expansive and spacious. Positive thinking is not enough to set us free. True joy comes through wholeness, welcoming every part of us home, not ignoring our suffering or fixating on it.

I AM WEARY OF religion. But I am also weary of my addictions, the physical ways I try to escape my soul wound. At first, my daily drinking and revolving door of lovers feels like a legitimate pursuit of pleasure. It is part of the culture I am immersed in, and it feels liberating to rebel against the restrictions of my religious past.

But it turns into an emotional dependency, a way to temporarily relieve my anxiety and depression. Of course, relying on alcohol and casual sex to alter my mood only amplifies my struggle.

I feel trapped and need an escape, but this is not the freedom I crave. My addictions are another false narrative to protect me from feeling what I do not want to feel.

The more I meditate, the less I want to drink. I don't enjoy showing up on the cushion with a hangover. The contrast is striking. At night, I am getting drunk, sleeping with men who desire me, but do not have the capacity to love me, and in the morning waking up and dragging myself to class.

Slowly, meditation seduces me. My practice is gentle and gradually more consistent. Witnessing my own patterns awakens me to this truth: I don't want to settle for little moments of physical pleasure, distractions, and escapes. I want, as I had always wanted, to be free.

My spiritual birthright is far more blissful than this shadow dance: another pretty, oblivious man in my bed, another round of drinks, another concert to drown out the sound of the primal music inside of me.

I decide to quit drinking for a year. I stop all at once and don't tell anyone about my decision. I immediately notice that I can't tolerate dating the men in my life without drinking, so I also stop dating and avoid the bars.

This sabbatical ends in a brief rendezvous with a doctor. Michael has a deep voice and empathetic brown eyes. When we are apart, he sends me love letters and poems. He is a generous, thoughtful man who takes me on a luxurious trip to Northern California after we date for a few months.

I wake up in our romantic bed-and-breakfast on the Pacific Coast and discover a delicate turquoise ring waiting for me on the table. Michael knows it is my favorite stone. His gentle, consistent presence provides a respite from my usual cycle of dating insanity.

I am not ready to be in a committed relationship or to even speak about my past, so we part ways. But I learn that it is possible for me to date a kind, healthy man. I also learn that in order to create the relationship I desire, I have to finally heal my trauma. My previous partners have been a reflection of my own divided mind. I want to return to wholeness.

When I walk away from our relationship, I devote myself fully to my own recovery. I make a commitment to myself: I will do whatever it takes to find healing and liberation. I choose to put my recovery first, above all else.

WITHOUT ALCOHOL OR casual sex, I feel extremely raw and vulnerable. But I also feel more like myself, or who I remember myself to be at a soul level. I reach out to a support group for survivors of childhood sexual abuse and start attending group therapy.

This warm, compassionate community of women makes it safe for me to share my truth. It is the first time I open up to other survivors and feel I don't have to carry my pain alone.

We discuss different ways to address common challenges in recovery, such as how to use grounding techniques when we are triggered or experiencing flashbacks. I appreciate that we don't discuss our past trauma stories in detail, but focus on tools for resilience in the present.

We acknowledge that we were impacted by the past but don't recount or relive our pain over and over again. I meet a fascinating designer in our circle who writes poetry and collects different kinds of salt.

Elena is passionate about urban design and social justice. She is my first soul friend in Boulder, someone I can deeply connect with and trust. We meet in coffee shops and the teahouse, sharing poetry, stories, and our passion for feminist activism. Our conversations help me remember who I am.

I don't need anyone else's religious traditions to mediate my experience of reality. I also don't need alcohol or soulless sex to distract me from my truth. My spiritual hunger is holy. So are the desires of my body. But I refuse to settle for illusions, the stories others tell me about what freedom means.

Poet Octavio Paz wrote, "Love is where desire and reality meet." My pursuit of desire without reality led me away from love. I need to let my sexual desires dance with the reality of my emotional truth, my core needs.

From religious fundamentalism to addiction, from conformity to rebellion, I had plunged into extremes, and neither extreme honored my deepest needs. Both of these extremes created false selves, armor to conceal my vulnerability. What I want is to know myself as sacred, whole, and free: in every dimension of my humanity. I want to be an undivided woman.

MEDITATION, MY SURVIVOR group, sobriety, and creative writing help me process and channel the pain I am carrying. I write a series of poems called "The Goddess Cycle" based on the myths of four goddesses: Athena, Aphrodite, Persephone, and Artemis.

I imagine they arrive in human form during modern times and work in the sex industry. Athena is a porn director. Aphrodite is the porn star. Persephone is the live performer/stripper, and Artemis is in charge of lights and props.

I research the symbols and subtleties of each of their myths to integrate into the poetic narrative. Each archetype has her own distinct personality and voice, her way of interpreting the objectification of women, as well as her expression of gender and sexuality. Although they work in the sex industry, each one has her own social critique of what is really happening.

I work on this series while I am taking a workshop with renowned Beat poet Anne Waldman. I read her work as a teen and love her dramatic energy and seer-like gaze. In a written review, she tells me my poetry is "forceful" and she is excited to "witness my powers as a performer and poet." Her handwritten note is a lifeline. I feel seen, heard, and respected as a writer.

I also have the privilege of taking workshops with the luminous Akilah Oliver, Tisa Bryant, and poetry priestess Danielle Vogel, all brilliant teachers and forces of nature. They each encourage me as a poet and create a vital space for new work to emerge.

Three pieces prove to be most significant for me at this time: "Kore of the Incantation," "Frida" (my tribute to Frida Kahlo), and "border girls," part of a series I write in honor of the murdered and disappeared women of Juárez, Mexico.

After revising my work in class, I submit several poems to a poetry competition at the University of Wisconsin–Madison and win first prize. I am elated. I've won literary awards before, but this is different. I receive a significant amount of money, and I am featured in *Poets and Writers* magazine, a publication I've read since I was a little girl, daydreaming in bookstores.

When I was nine I wrote on the first page of a new diary, "I aspire to be a professional writer." This award signals a transition to becoming the professional writer I wanted to be as a child. I am writing honestly, in my own voice, and am being acknowledged for my work.

I address murder, rape, sexual exploitation, and creative resilience in this series. I am not writing what I think others want to hear. I am writing exactly what I need to say.

I take the prize money and independently publish my third collection of poems, *Kore of the Incantation*. I don't feel compelled to seek out a publisher. I need to excavate and compile the work to make sense of my past.

I have already gathered a couple hundred poems and don't want to have to limit the scope or content of the book. Sifting through my pieces, reading every line composed during my time in Boulder and earlier work from Austin, I feel I am collecting fragments of myself, remembering what has been dismembered and cast aside.

Many of the poems are a surprise to me. I don't remember writing them, so every time I look through my pages, I rediscover and recover a forgotten part. The collection closes with a poem addressed to my trafficker, called "sacred siren." It is an affirmation of my true spiritual identity, a reclamation of power, and a severing of our energetic ties.

I am ready to face the past and write my own narrative, to move beyond the spell of addiction and the illusion of religious certainty into the wise, wild mystery of healing.

i am not the violence
you forced on this body divine,
my clear bell & shrine,
of the first singer sounding sunrise.

i am becoming the author
of my own story, definer of days,
creatrix and sage. the art of this incantation
wakes to a wave as i glide to the other side

of the first divide,
taking refuge in my glad origin,
purging the root of the poison
to soak in the nectar of a new day.

you cannot un-create the spirit spark.
i am disarming your mad prophecies
with quiet gestures of kindness.
i am the breath of ecstasy.

& you do not possess the power to define me,
confine my wet dervish
or tame the torrent of the sacred siren.
you define yourself by what you do.

i no longer grieve for the man
you could have been
before you stifled the tender hunger
of the child within.

you have made your decision
& i make mine
as my razor strikes through
the night-drenched umbilicus between us.

may my voice remind you
of the life you have forsaken,
the cleansing waterfall
behind the ancient wall.

may my voice remind you
of the life that loved you into being,
the life you will never succeed
in breaking.

This collection signals my first step to openly acknowledging my history of abuse and is the first time I address my abuser directly in a piece of writing. I am making the invisible visible and turning the unspeakable into song.

I publish my book just before I meet Gabriel, the man who would reveal to me where I most needed to heal.

All that is still unconscious in me is incarnated in him.

chapter seven

Take Refuge

This is live or die
And I won't lie like this
Just to get my little fix.

THE FIRST NIGHT I MEET GABRIEL, he kisses me on the cheek. Our eccentric designer friend Vaughn introduces us, insisting we will love each other. Gabriel plays acoustic guitar and sings for me in an old warehouse our friend converted into his art studio.

His green eyes brighten as his soulful voice fills the vast room, echoing off concrete floors and high ceilings. The space is empty except for a sofa, a couple of chairs, large canvases propped against the wall, and a screen printer.

"We should have an open mic here," he says.

"Absolutely," I agree.

"We can easily build a stage and set it up in that corner," he says.

"I know musicians and poets we can invite. I would love to host one here," I reply.

Gabriel is handsome and charismatic. He looks like he belongs on the beach with his shoulder-length hair, tall athletic build, and tan skin. Everywhere he goes, women adore him. I do not. At least, not in the beginning.

There is a streak of arrogance I sense in him, as well as a need to prove himself. But I also recognize his creative genius. He pursues and charms me.

He tells me I am different, not like the other women he knows, the desperate ones who follow him around after shows.

One night, when I am dropping him off after a gig, he turns to me and says, "I think you might be my wife."

I laugh. "I think you've had too much to drink. Go inside."

I believe we will just remain friends, but Gabriel persuades me to be with him through his constant adoration and persistence. I *am* attracted to him, and he makes me feel valuable. I see him turn down so many other women who throw themselves at him. He constantly affirms me and makes me feel safe, desired, and worth pursuing.

We start dating, and he quickly moves into my place. We enjoy a wild, passionate year together: playing music, making love, recording songs, and hosting parties for our artist friends. We can be silly together, crack absurd jokes, and talk about spirituality all in the same conversation.

After a few months of dating, though, I notice he is drinking more and more. What starts out as a few drinks and maybe a couple of hits of weed turns into regular all-night benders with hard liquor. He stumbles into the bedroom rambling incoherently and wakes me up, insisting there is something we need to discuss.

In the morning, he doesn't remember anything that happened. In his sober hours, we talk over coffee and trade stories about our families. Gabriel is a veteran and has a history of child abuse. He tells me about how his father beat him so severely as a child that he came to school with massive bruises and he was taken from his family for a while.

Eventually, his mom came for him, but he was deeply wounded and already felt abandoned by her for leaving him with his abusive father.

I confide in him about my experience of child sex trafficking, how I am on a healing path and struggle with PTSD, intrusive memories, and nightmares. The wounded child in me can see the wounded child in him. We were both violently abused. We are singers, songwriters, and artists. We find solace in animals, nature, and creative expression.

We both grew up in the South, within traditions of conservative Christianity. We are deeply spiritual, yet hurt by the church. We also both turned to alcohol for self-medication. It is a recipe for deep connection and chaos.

IT WOULD BE easy to paint an image of Gabriel as a monster, to describe every cruel word and deed. But he is merely a man, a brokenhearted, romantic, creative, inspiring, angry, grandiose, and occasionally sadistic man.

His addictions fuel his internal conflicts and rage. My codependency keeps me disconnected from my own pain and focused on caring for him. My vision of love is distorted. I believe my devotion requires relentless sacrifice at all costs.

When Gabriel screams at me, I see the lost child within him, and he uses my empathy against me. In the beginning, I think he loses control of his temper. Yet over time, I observe a pattern. He is far more calculating. Gabriel rarely reveals this part of himself in public. He can immediately turn it off, if someone shows up.

I am calm in the face of his anger and often think, "This is not about me. He must be in a lot of pain to do this." In the ultimate sense, that is true. Gabriel's rage is a reflection of his own inner world, not of me. But it is, also, about me, because his choices impact my well-being, my ability to feel safe and sacred in my own body.

He hates how calm I am when he is in the midst of a tirade. "Grow a fucking spine!" he yells in my face, telling me I am weak for not fighting back.

"You have no idea how much strength this takes," I reply quietly.

My refusal to escalate the situation usually leads to him walking off in a fury and soothing himself with a cigarette.

In a way, he plays out the best and worst of my childhood. The adoration I received from my family, the joy of music, the playfulness of adventures with my brothers, as well as the cruel attacks of my trafficker. He embodies in a single day what is still not integrated in me, the extremes of a childhood filled with warmth, love, *and* abuse. He can be highly affectionate until his internal landscape shifts.

I learned as a child that love meant laying down your life for others. Through false interpretations of this teaching, I believed I should be the sacrifice and place my body on the altar of "compassion," no matter what the price. But I am learning that my compassion is incomplete because it does not include me. My sacrifice is self-abandonment and self-neglect disguised as unconditional love. I need a love that honors me, too.

He usually hides his severe outbursts from others, but one night he refuses to conceal his rage, and the police intervene. We are out at a bar for drinks. Gabriel goes over to talk to a few guys and then disappears.

He has a habit of wandering off to look for drugs or other trouble, so I don't pay attention. After I finish sipping a glass of red wine, I notice he has been gone longer than usual. I ask one of the bouncers if he has seen my boyfriend.

"He got kicked out," he says.

"Why?" I ask.

"For starting a fight," he replies.

I walk outside to check on him, and he is seething. He immediately starts yelling at me, "Where were you?"

He is furious that I stayed inside after he was kicked out. I explain that I didn't know what happened and just found out.

"You should have known. You just left me out here by myself. They wouldn't let me back in," he rages.

"I'm sorry. I didn't know. The bouncer just told me. Let's go."

As he recounts what happened at the bar, he keeps yelling. We are walking in the middle of the street. I am embarrassed and try to guide him away from the crowd.

A block later he is still screaming. This time at me. I stop by a tree and start crying. "Why are you crying? What's wrong with you? You're going to get us in trouble," he shouts.

"Leave me alone," I say, tired of being yelled at.

I can't stop crying, and my tears enrage him.

A young man walking by stops to check on me.

"Are you okay?" he asks gently. "Do you need help?"

Gabriel storms over, trying to intimidate him and get him to leave.

The young man is resolute. He stays. "What are you doing to this poor girl?" He can see I am in pain.

"You need to leave us the fuck alone," Gabriel yells.

"Do you need a ride somewhere?" he offers, ignoring Gabriel.

Other people on the street watch the whole scene and call the police.

By the time they arrive, Gabriel has walked off. The officers say they have received a call and need to talk to my boyfriend.

"Where is he?" they ask.

"I think he went back to the hotel where we are staying," I say.

"Do you want a ride?"

"Yes," I reply.

It is late and I don't want to walk back by myself, so I am grateful for the ride. We arrive at the hotel room door together. When Gabriel opens the door, he is calm and agreeable. One officer asks, "Is everything okay? We got a call."

"Yes, officer. Everything is fine. We just had too much to drink," Gabriel says.

"We received a complaint for disturbing the peace, so try to keep it down."

"No problem," Gabriel says as I walk inside.

"Take care. You have a good night," the officer says.

As soon as Gabriel shuts the door, he looks at me as if he wants to kill me. He screams at me, "You worthless piece of shit! You worthless piece of shit! You threw me under the bus. I hate you."

I quickly walk past him and sit on the edge of the bed. "Why are you saying that? I love you," I plead through my tears.

His eyes turn cold. There is no light in them. "Why did you bring the cops here?" he yells.

"I didn't. They said they were coming and offered me a ride."

He rushes to the bed, pins down my shoulders, and climbs on top of me, screaming in my face again, "You worthless piece of shit! I despise you! I should destroy you!" When I try to get away, he grabs me and throws me into a dresser. I drop to the floor and collapse, sobbing.

Right after this, we hear a knock at the door. It is the police again. One of the hotel guests called them because they overheard Gabriel screaming. They take Gabriel to a separate room and come back to question me. I am still trembling in a fetal position on the floor when they ask me, "What happened? Did he hurt you?" I am too raw and shocked to lie and cover for him. I tell the truth.

"Are you afraid of him?" one of the officers asks gently.

"Yes." I am terrified. I am not thinking about him going to jail. I just know I am no longer safe.

*G*ABRIEL IS HELD in jail for several days. A "No-Contact Order" is issued, but Gabriel calls me from jail anyway. He apologizes and says he is going to get sober and start going to Alcoholics Anonymous. He promises to change and focus on his recovery. I am hurt, but I believe him. I don't want to leave. I want him to heal and become the man I thought I fell in love with.

Instead of pressing charges and pushing for jail time, I recommend to the judge that he be given the opportunity for a drug and alcohol treatment program. Due to my testimony, his charges are lowered from domestic violence to disturbing the peace. I protect my abuser.

Gabriel is put on probation, has to attend AA, and takes random drug and alcohol tests. After he comes home from jail, he works hard to convince me that he is sorry and he will do everything he can to make amends. He is sober for a few months, and then his anger surfaces again.

The old patterns return. I ask him if he would consider seeing a doctor to talk about his depression, anxiety, and anger. He agrees. After Gabriel describes his symptoms, the doctor says, "I think you have what is called intermittent explosive disorder."

"What are the treatment options for that?" I ask.

"Usually therapy and potentially antianxiety drugs," he says.

Gabriel refuses to go to therapy or take any drugs. He claims his newfound sobriety and AA are enough. "Anyway, I don't think I have that," he says.

"You show some of the symptoms of PTSD," I say. "Why won't you talk to a counselor?"

"I tried that before. It didn't work," he replies.

His destructive behavior escalates again. When he is upset, he threatens to take my new terrier puppy and drop him off "somewhere you will never find him." One day, he steals my car, credit card, and dog and disappears to another state as a way of punishing me. Another time he takes my car, I have to jump out of the way so he won't hit me.

My adorable pup Rio is my greatest joy. He sleeps snuggled up by my belly each night. Feeling his tiny body breathing into mine is one of my few comforts. When Gabriel screams at me, Rio hides behind my legs, shaking. This pushes me over the edge.

I finally start to consider leaving him. After he refuses therapy and medication and threatens to take my dog from me, I can see this will only end in more destruction. Gabriel claims he wants help, but he refuses to face his trauma and mental illness.

I decide to focus on my writing and apply for a summer writing program in Kenya. I need to return to myself, to *my* desires. I need to feel that my life belongs to me.

Gabriel's insatiable anger is consuming me. As soon as I feel he is making progress, the beast wakes and I am left searching for another remedy, another way to help him recover.

His sickness has become my own. I have to break the cycle of codependency, but I don't know how. I only know I have lost myself trying to save him from the pain of his past and created more suffering by resolving to love him despite all the damage to myself.

I wait for an evening when he is in a good mood after AA.

"I was accepted into a writing program in Kenya. I am going to Nairobi for a few weeks," I reveal, bracing myself for an explosion.

"When do you leave?" he says calmly.

"Next month."

"Okay. I wish you wouldn't leave me," he says.

"This will give you time to focus on your recovery and spend time with the guys. They'll look out for you," I offer.

"Yeah," he says flatly.

Gabriel acts so peaceful about my trip. It is eerie. For the first time in more than a year, I feel like I am making a decision for *myself*, and *only myself*, to honor my desires as a writer and a woman. It is a step toward leaving his chaotic dance behind and listening to my own wisdom. She is telling me, "It's time to leave."

I MEET HABIBA, A native Kenyan writer, by the hotel pool in Nairobi. She looks like a dancer with her black hair swept up into a bun. Her floral blouse and long skirt gently move in the wind as she sips a glass of white wine. Habiba's brown skin shines with dark amber tones in the fading light of sunset. I am drawn in by her inviting presence and melodic voice.

"What are you passionate about?" I ask.

"Creative writing is my passion," she says. "I am writing a novel about the journey of a Somali refugee. I want to travel to Somalia for research, but I am concerned for my safety."

I ask her about the new, revised constitution in Kenya and how this has affected life for women there. Once again, her face brightens. She says, "The constitution was very dated. Now it favors women."

"How do Kenyan women feel about this?" I ask.

She smiles. "I think they are very happy to have equal opportunity."

Her friend Nancy, also a native Kenyan, joins us at the poolside table with a glass of red wine. When I tell her I am passionate about the issues of sexual assault and domestic violence, she says, "Gender violence is a big problem here. We have a Gender Violence Center in Nairobi. You hear things on the news like a thirty-year-old raping a five-year-old. Do you have that in your country? I don't know why, but I think it's getting worse."

"Even with the development and affluence of the United States, gender violence is still a significant problem," I explain.

"How many women are affected?" she asks.

"One out of six women are survivors of sexual assault and one out of four women are survivors of domestic violence."

"That surprises me," she says.

Nancy expresses concern about the struggles of girls in her country. She tells me about the girls she works with as a counselor: the girl in the slums whose mother works as a prostitute in their tiny one-room shanty because it is the only way she can feed the family; the girl who is a gifted performer, yet struggles with low self-esteem and suicidal thoughts; the girl she took to the hospital at fifteen with severe complications from a self-induced abortion; the girls who drop out of school because of an abusive boyfriend, early pregnancy, or forced marriage.

"I think women are the strongest people in the world," she says. As she pours another glass of wine, Nancy speaks passionately about the need for change, particularly for all young women to be educated and have access to family planning resources. "Most people think that help is going to come from the West, but I think it is important for our generation to recognize our history and create change."

As I listen to Habiba and Nancy, I am inspired by their courage and creativity. They are honest about the realities of social injustice in their country, but confident they can create new stories, new ways for their voices to be heard. Since the passing of the revised constitution, women must account for at least one-third of Parliament. Abortion is now legal when a medical expert determines that the life of the mother is at stake. Funding for women's health care has been greatly expanded.

My Kenyan sisters acknowledge the devastating elements of their country's history and the violent aftershocks of colonialism. But they are not just survivors. They are creators, boldly writing their own narrative.

A COUPLE OF DAYS later, I take a small plane to the island of Lamu, just off the coast of Kenya. The turquoise water of the Indian Ocean circles the shore, and the sunlight spills across brightly painted homes.

There are no cars on the island. The locals use donkeys to carry their goods and handmade sailboats to navigate the surrounding territories. Children run free and play together, singing, smiling, and shouting, "Jambo! Jambo!" Swahili for "Hello."

A few of the little girls follow me from their games at the seaside as I explore shops with exquisite bead necklaces and vivid batiks. A nine-year-old with braids tells me she loves English and talks about her school. She is bright and inquisitive.

"What is your favorite part of school?" I ask.

"*Me!*" she shouts with a wide smile.

I laugh.

"*You* are your favorite part of school? That's wonderful. You should always feel that way!"

We walk side by side, along the narrow dirt lanes between shops. Men lead their donkeys past us, carrying crates of food and crafts to sell.

"What are your dreams for the future?" I ask.

"I want to finish my education, so I can help my family. I want to be a doctor," she says proudly.

"I love that. You will be an excellent doctor."

She smiles confidently, and I can see she still loves herself.

When she runs off to play with her friends, I offer a silent prayer for her, a prayer for protection, a prayer that she will be kept safe and never lose her sense of worth. She is joyful and without shame, as all girls should be.

I WAKE IN A hotel room with white curtains stirring in the breeze. I sit with a cup of coffee and my journal on the balcony overlooking the ocean, watching the sailboats pass. I am serene and enchanted by the rhythm of the waves.

I came to the island for a writing seminar with powerful poet Cornelius Eady. I feel more at home than I have for many years. I meet with our group on the rooftop of a house, a small tribe of adventurous writers who are gathered to study with him, experience Kenyan culture, and learn from native poets, musicians, and artists.

On a sun-drenched, clear afternoon, we set sail on a sleek wood sailboat, handmade by local artisans. One of the sailors plays Bob Marley songs on his acoustic guitar. Another joins in with a small drum. I sing along when they hit the chorus of "No Woman, No Cry."

When we arrive at the quiet beach, there are no children, no donkeys, and no sounds of trade. Only sweeping stretches of pristine white sand and pink stucco cottages lacing the terrain. After an afternoon of swimming in the sea and lounging in the sun, we gather for a meal and share our writing. Through poems and stories, we share the same irresistible instinct: to fashion form out of the raw material of our wayward lives and loves, to feed ourselves with the music of words.

When it is my turn to share a poem, I sing the opening lines, with the sound of the waves as my backing band. An invocation and remembrance of my primal power, of who I am without him.

be careful with a woman like me
who lives like a drunkard
for the grey honey of the sea
who sends her singing voice to distant coves
like a hurricane trapped in a green bottle just to see
if shrouds can be ripped & the dead raised.

be careful with a woman like me
who sharpens her heart like an ivory dagger
& howls her monsoon music to the moon
who wraps her secrets in silver cloths
to hide beneath deck & makes no promises

who is a cloud no hammer can nail to the bed
who will keep you restless & well fed on blackberries.

be careful with a woman like me
who dances in with a brass band
then slips away like a line in the sand
when the slightest wind moves.

it is not that i can't be true.
it is not that you are a red lacquered door
to open & quickly pass through.

but what appears to be
a delicate locket hanging
from a gold chain at my neck
holds a private tempest & the shipwreck
of every storm-torn night my skin eats.

be careful of a woman like me.
i am true the way rain is true.
i am pure & vanishing.
when the thirst of brittle leaves is quenched
when the land is a screaming emerald
it is clear. i am no longer here.

i am as restless as a sloop at bay,
swaying with the seducing wave & her dark granite gaze.
i secretly flunked the school of manners
though i held my spoon at such a graceful angle.

i disguised my dissent behind the careful lifting
of the teacup & memorized the map of their make believe.

i breathed heavy in the bed of my enemy
so i could overturn the twist of the sordid fist.
i oiled the gears of my mind like a pleasing machine.

you should be careful with a woman like me.
all the while i trained in guerilla warfare
chewed rabid stew, sank my teeth
into the neck of a god who does not topple
at the earthquake of the shrine.

i crossed seven purple mountains on my knees.
i sucked on stones until they turned to bread.
i gave my heart to the hungry to eat for breakfast
& you will find only the grey honey of the sea
rocking, rocking
in a woman like me.

I hide the abuse from my family and friends just as I did as a child. I feel ashamed I am in this position and not ready to ask for help. But after Kenya, I can feel myself distancing from Gabriel. I tell him I want to go home, so I can spend time with my parents.

One night I am riding in the car with my mom when he calls. As soon as I answer the phone, he starts screaming. I can't even tell why he is upset. It is so loud my mom can hear. He won't stop, so I hang up the phone.

"What was that?" she asks.

"Oh, he always talks like that," I reply.

"I don't like anyone who speaks to my daughter that way," she says sharply.

I sigh.

"He should never talk to you like that. Not even once," she says.

I can see how disturbed she is. What has become a part of my daily life is clearly wrong and unacceptable. It wakes me up to see how upset it makes her. It is only one phone call. I have been living with this for two years.

Over the next few days, I share more about what my life is like with Gabriel. I tell her about the arrest, the physical and verbal abuse, his threats, jealousy, all the ways he isolated me and convinced me I should never talk about our issues. "It only makes it worse," he would tell me. "It's no one else's business."

"Mom, he even told me he didn't want me singing anymore be-cause he thought I would cheat on him if I played out with a band. Every time I put on makeup and wear something beautiful, he gets upset. He thinks I'm trying to get attention from other men."

Horrified, she encourages me to leave.

When I see him, he knows something has shifted.

"What did you talk about with your mom?"

"We were just catching up."

"Did you talk about us?"

"A little bit."

"Did you tell her about the arrest?"

"Yes."

"I told you to never tell them about that," he screams. "If they try anything with me, I will kill them."

"What are you talking about?"

He stares at me with intense hatred. "You know I've killed people before," he says coldly.

"That was the military," I say.

"You've ruined everything. Your parents will never look at me the same. This is all your fault. I told you not to talk about our problems. You know my first wife—her mom tried to talk down to me once. I picked her up and threw her across the room."

I don't tell him I want to leave. I know it isn't safe. So, I wait for the right moment, a moment he would never expect, so I can disappear and never see him again.

The next day, we are heading to the grocery store. He is still upset I told my mom about the abuse. Gabriel suddenly pulls the car over and says, "If you ever cross me again, I will beat you to death. You betrayed me. Just when you think I've forgotten all about it, I will show up and ruin your life."

I say nothing, keeping still and staring straight ahead, hoping he will not hit me. When we return to our apartment, I keep my distance and plan my next move. The following day, I tell him I am going to go to my older brother's house and will be gone for a few hours.

I take the essentials: my sweet dog and laptop with all my writing. Everything else I can live without. As I walk out the door, I tell him good-bye for the last time. With Rio in my arms and one bag on my shoulder, I disappear into the Hill Country night. Gabriel will never see me or speak to me again.

When I arrive at my brother's place, we sit on the back porch, and I tell him the truth.

"No one should ever treat you that way. You can stay here as long as you want," he offers.

"Thanks, Brother."

We both cry.

"If he ever puts his hands on you again, I'll kill him," he says in between swigs of beer. "You deserve so much better."

"I know," I say, and almost believe it. "I love you."

"I love you, too, Sis."

chapter eight

Searching for Persephone

I'm searching for Persephone.
The sacred child inside of me.
She is weeping tears of gold.
She is the one I must hold.

He stole her to his underground.
Thought she could be the remedy.
Bound her to his bed of thorns.
But she's made for different alchemy.

M Y MOTHER LINE IS FIERCE AND tender, filled with both devastating trauma and powerful gifts. I am the fourth generation in a line that has been given spiritual sight. I imagine this inner knowing has been with us far longer.

The gift of the seer, the gift of witness, felt excruciating as a child. What was happening in both the realm of the flesh and the realm of the spirit made me want to bury my gift. I not only silenced my voice as a child. I also shut off my sight and forced the seer part of me underground.

I think of her as Persephone, the one taken captive by Hades in the ancient Greek myth, the sacred child separated from her mother, Demeter. My healing path is a descent into that hidden realm, to find her and bring her home. In the underworld, I can still see everything: all the abuse; the ancestral trauma; the grief of my mother; the pain of my grandmother Marjorie, whom I call "Grammy"; the haunted eyes of my great-grandmother Zora.

I also see the legacy of creativity: Zora, a painter and photographer; Marjorie, a poet and songwriter; and my mother, a spiritual teacher and writer.

My Grammy lives an adventurous life and encourages me to fearlessly explore the world. She plays acoustic guitar, sings folk songs with her rich, deep voice, and lived on a sailboat for several years off the coast of Seattle when I was a child. She embarked on scuba-diving trips across South America and Indonesia many years ago when few women explored the ocean.

Grammy is passionate, brilliant, and witty. She studied English at Rice University as a young woman and cannot resist correcting everyone's grammar. She tells hilarious stories about her adventures and former partners.

"Oh, dahhhling, my first husband was handsome, but he was dull as dishwater. I had to propose that we create one world government at dinner parties just to spark debate. Of course, I didn't actually believe in it, but if I hadn't enlivened the conversation, I would have died of boredom," Grammy moans.

"They wanted all the women to go to a separate room and talk about children and cooking. I wouldn't do it. He would get so angry and say, 'You are embarrassing me.' Ha! At least I wasn't *boring*," she says playfully.

Grammy also claims she is a direct descendant of Lady Godiva. With her wild, rebellious spirit, it is easy to believe. When she was a model in Houston, she agreed to be a part of a PR stunt to help sell diamonds for the Diamond Guild.

She went to the opera decked out in a lavish diamond necklace and earrings. That night they publicly announced that the jewels had been stolen. The story of this "crime" and her disappearing diamonds appeared in the *Houston Chronicle* the next day.

She adores the theater and acted professionally in off-Broadway productions before she had children. Her love of theatrics never fades. Grammy insists that all her grandchildren serenade her with songs. Most of us write music, which pleases her immensely. She fills her house with crystals, shells, and fabrics she collects from her travels. Volumes of poetry and classic novels line her shelves.

Grammy channels an almost religious devotion to intellectual pursuits, adventures, and all forms of art. She takes me to see a diverse range of live performances: from the musical *Rent* to Italian operas. My exposure to a wealth of creative culture has always been paramount to her.

Grammy gave me my first poetry book as a little girl, a blue volume of poems by Edna St. Vincent Millay. When I read a biography of Millay, I witnessed so much of my Grammy in her reckless, passionate life.

As editor for the *Houston Chronicle* newspaper and a gifted speaker, William Repass, Grammy's father, fought for social justice and supported organizations like the NAACP. At nineteen, she found him on the bathroom floor of their home after he shot himself in the head. Despite his wonderful contributions, my great-grandfather struggled with alcoholism and severe depression.

The loss of her father, whom she admired and adored, shaped the rest of her life. A part of her stays in perpetual mourning over him.

As a teenager, I gave her my first poetry collection, *defectors from eden*. When I read passages aloud to her, she said, "This is so powerful. My father would have loved this." We stared out the window of her home overlooking Lake Travis. "I wish you could have met him," she said dreamily.

In her fifties, Grammy fell in love with a married man named Bill. She called him "the love of my life." His wife, who was committed to a psychiatric ward, got a day pass to visit family. She shot Bill at point-blank range, and he died immediately.

The loss of her loves, her father and her partner, left her feeling alone in the world. Because Grammy carries herself with such bravado and charisma, it is easy for people to overlook her vulnerability.

As an actress and model in her youth, she knew how to captivate a crowd. But now, Grammy does not have a censor and occasionally makes random acerbic comments at family gatherings. Fortunately, I am never her target. When we are alone, she releases her armor and can be very gentle and contemplative.

During a family reunion by the Guadalupe River, I ask, "Is there anything you wish you had done differently with your life? Do you have any regrets?" She pauses for a moment, resting in a rocking chair, and takes a deep breath. "I wish your grandfather would have loved me."

Her response surprises me because she has always been so fiercely independent and passionate about her freedom. She does not want to answer to anyone. Yet deep within, Grammy still hungers to be loved. I don't think this is about her marriage and divorce from my grandfather. It seems to be about her core wound of abandonment, the story of being left behind by those she loves.

I never imagined Grammy would have a spiritual awakening as death approached. She has always been so defiant and resolute in her beliefs. But in her eighties, she announces in her usual dramatic fashion, "I have been *talking* to God." I try to act like this is a common pastime for her.

After years of conversation about spirituality and her adamant refusal to give up her identity as an agnostic, I am shocked. My mom also witnesses this proclamation. Grammy turns to us and says, "I want us to pray and sing together."

Again, we act as if she does this all the time. My mom and I offer prayers of gratitude and ask God to give her a revelation of Divine Love. We sing a cappella in a small circle, three voices, three generations, braided together in joy. We all hold each other and smile.

Then she announces, "We are so *powerful*."

I laugh. "Yes, we are."

After spending some time reading the New Testament again, she decides she is into Jesus. We both agree he treats women with love and dignity.

"But I still think Paul is a misogynist," she exclaims.

"I hear you," I respond.

We also chat about the fact that we should be able to call God "He" or "She" because God is Spirit anyway. "Forget the patriarchy!" I insist. She cackles, and I grin as we decide how it should be.

The last time I see my Grammy, she says what she always says when she greets me. In her most theatrical voice, she crows weakly, "Dahhhhling, is it really you?"

"Dahhhhling," I say, moving toward the bed to embrace her.

She holds my face in her soft, elegant hands, covered in exquisite wrinkles, and says gently, gazing into my eyes, "Brooke, you are *so* beautiful." We both tear up. She speaks directly into my soul.

"So are you, Grammy. I love you."

A few days later, she leaves her body. The dark chocolate and red wine I placed beside her bed was her last communion.

My GRAMMY PASSES just after I flee from Gabriel. I move into her home to hide from him and mourn her passing. When I arrive at her house, I see an envelope with my name written in her graceful script. I open the seal and discover she left behind several of her poems for me typed on beautiful parchment. The series was dedicated to her lost lover, Bill, the man she sailed with around the world.

As I read each line, I can feel her with me. She left other gifts for me: several crystals, a woven guitar strap from South America, a lapis ring, and her favorite book—an emerald green, leather-bound copy of *The Hobbit*. Each sacred object soothes me as I release my life with Gabriel and miss Grammy deeply.

For about a week, I curl up with Rio in bed, reading her poetry and journals, speaking to her spirit, wrapping myself in her blankets. I wear her jewelry, drink her wine, and explore her photography. She comforts me in her passing to the other side. I rest and grieve in this house where she departed from her body. But her spirit does not leave me.

Not an angel or a traditional grandmother, Grammy was one sassy crone. But her love, even after physical death, nourishes me in my time of mourning. One day when I am searching through her belongings, I find *defectors from eden*, the book I wrote as a teen and dedicated to her.

On the cover she appears as a toddler, wearing a long white cotton dress, gazing at the light on her porch. The inscription reads,

> Dear Grammy,
> Thank you for passing on the music of your courage and
> your love of the written word.
> I love you.
> Brooke

I also find another poem I published in my second collection, *daughter of the burning*, which is a tribute to the four generations of my maternal line. It is called "language of inheritance."

> *the lineage of these strange, solitary ones,*
> *those of us caught with a singing in the head,*
> *uncurls deep into the memory of my blood.*
>
> *zora, the painter, the hurricane chaser.*
> *marjorie, the actress, sculptor of selves, of words.*
> *& i, in the echo of years*
> *with a knife in my belly*
> *& the inevitable candle at my voice-box,*
> *study the unfinished portrait of my mama,*
> *age 9, all pastel & singing & wounds.*
>
> *if i believe in our darkness,*
> *i must believe in our luminosity, too.*

i keep clawing for the kingdom,
the invisible bread, homesick
like margritte's black-winged angel
on that mute-grey city bridge.
with many rough edges,
dark, chosen burdens,
we may stumble like songs
that are never fully written.

all play party to this war
against music, against light,
not knowing which side is which
or what little deaths to permit,
always assuming that we possess
perfect pitch.

there are moments for instruction
And there are moments for blood.
We unite through the shared opening
of these soul veins, whispering
"these are my ruins, my holy rhythms,
these are my belting hungers
& hidden promiscuities,
perhaps we could uncover
a method to redeem."

or wake to what is
& incite what should be.

we will
& of course we will,
those of us struck with a nourishing burden
of a singing in the head.

I intuitively understand that healing my personal trauma is connected to healing the trauma of my maternal line. I do not know where to begin or how to create a safe space to witness all the darkness and luminosity, all the hunger and music in our blood. Yet I know this wild, wise inheritance refuses to be silenced any longer.

AFTER I LIVE in my grandmother's home for a couple of weeks, I talk with my mom.

"How are you?" she asks gently.

"I am in pain, and I don't know how to heal myself."

"I think you should get counseling at Safe Place," she offers.

"I am so tired of counseling. It never helps me," I respond.

"I think you should try one more time. Please consider going. I'll take you if you want me to."

"I suppose it couldn't hurt at this point. I don't know what else to do," I say.

I know about Safe Place, their domestic violence shelter and counseling services. My mom, her stepmom Patti, and my cousin Eloise generously donate their time and money to support Safe Place's work helping survivors of sexual assault and domestic violence. I never reached out to them in the past because I thought they only worked with adult survivors of more recent assaults.

Even my mother, who volunteers with Safe Place as a speaker and educator, bravely sharing her own story of childhood sexual abuse, was not aware they offered support for adults who experienced sex trafficking as children. Although they are well respected and a vital part of our community, we didn't understand how they might be able to help me. But after I experience domestic violence, we recognize a path forward in receiving support there.

I am desperate for help, the day my mom takes me to Safe Place. Because of so many negative experiences with therapy and self-proclaimed "spiritual counselors," I have lost heart.

After driving past the outer security gate on the property, we walk to the front door, where I confirm my name and appointment. They screen everyone carefully. So many of their clients are at risk for further abuse and, in some cases, at risk for being murdered by their former partners. They let me through the second gate, and I am guided to a small room for my intake appointment.

The blond, blue-eyed male intake counselor appears to be in his early thirties. I feel my stomach clench and chest tighten when I see him. I do not want to talk to a man about my abuse history. But his gentle manner makes me feel safe.

"Do you currently feel threatened? Do you have a safe place to stay?" he asks.

"I am staying at my grandmother's place. He doesn't know about her home, so I feel physically safe for now. I got a new phone number and email, so he can't communicate with me. Right now, I need counseling."

"We can get you into counseling, but there is a three-month wait list." He explains that like most domestic violence shelters, Safe

Place is always inundated with requests for counseling and does not have all the funding necessary to meet that demand.

So, I have to wait.

The intake counselor remains thoughtful and supportive as we discuss safety planning. "What will you do if Gabriel shows up?" he asks. "Do you want to file a restraining order?"

"A restraining order won't help," I explain. "He's been ordered not to see me or contact me. He doesn't care. I think I just need to stay where I am and not give him any access to me. The last message I sent him was an email saying that if he didn't leave me alone, I would call the police. Then I blocked the account."

Speaking about the logistics of my safety feels surreal, as if I am speaking about another woman's life. Before I met Gabriel, I was determined to put my recovery first. I reached out to the support group in Boulder for survivors of childhood sexual abuse and discovered healing tools like meditation. These steps were vital, but without long-term, trauma-informed therapy, I was still vulnerable to being drawn back into a cycle of abuse.

Gabriel embodied all that was not yet integrated in my own psyche. My unconscious mind cast him as the charismatic yet cruel actor in the shadow play of my life. We re-created scenes, so familiar to me, scenes of abandonment and betrayal, scenes of intense adoration and sadistic violence.

He both worshipped me and took pleasure ripping me from the throne he built for me.

This dance of shadows ended with an intervention from another powerful character in my unconscious mind, my mother. In the original trauma of being separated from her and violently exploited, no one witnessed my pain. No one intervened. I felt invisible and my suffering unspeakable.

Now, as an adult woman, my mother witnessed my pain and guided me to safety. She had always loved me, but she wasn't there physically when I needed her most as a seven-year-old child.

This, of course, was not her fault. Though a devoted and nurturing mother, when she returned from the hospital, she interpreted my sadness and silences as a consequence of her illness and absence, not a sign of abuse.

Concerned about some of the shifts she noticed in my personality, she took me to a child psychologist. I did not like or trust the therapist. I felt in my stomach that I was just being watched, not loved or truly seen. I remember playing with a dollhouse and being acutely aware that she was observing me, looking for clues. When I asked my mom about this time, she told me the psychologist said, "Brooke will be fine. She's very resilient."

The story of our separation stayed with me all these years, guiding and haunting me. In many ways, I became fused with her, wanting to be near her always, wanting to be like her in every way.

My relationship with Gabriel played out like a reenactment of the story of Demeter, who loses her daughter to Hades. The first time I was violently forced into the underworld, my mother did not know. There was no witness, no searching for the lost child.

How could she know to search for me when she did not know I was missing?

So, part of me, the wounded daughter, her Persephone, stayed in hiding until Hades appeared in another form. The second time, he appeared as he appeared in my childhood, with blond hair and hungry eyes, full of promises that were only lies. He dragged me back to the underworld. Just when I thought his hold on me was finally broken, Hades forced me to remember that he was still master over a part of my psyche. My trafficker reincarnated as my abuser, so the story could continue.

I descended again and found my way to her, my Sacred Child. I am discovering I have to become the mother I needed most, so I can guide her safely home. My mom can encourage me in my recovery, but she cannot be the one to descend into the darkness and take the hand of my Persephone. Instead of being forced underground, I am now consciously choosing my descent with a powerful healing intention. This homecoming starts with a return to the wisdom of my body.

AFTER THREE MONTHS of waiting, I receive a call letting me know I can begin therapy. In my first session with Kristin Hensley, a highly intuitive and gifted therapist, I share all the major traumatic events of my life. She doesn't ask me to, but I am ready to disclose every-thing and finally be witnessed. In an uncensored outpouring of pain, I tell her about the child sex trafficking, domestic violence, both brain injuries, and religious abuse.

I hold nothing back—becoming completely vulnerable.

I also share with her how some therapists and spiritual counselors I have seen were not trained to work with complex sexual trauma. I explain how these practices, which weren't evidence based or eth-ical, retraumatized me. I talk about how I want help, but have lost hope after so many disappointments.

I instinctively trust her from the moment I meet her. A soft light seems to surround her, and I feel her deep empathy. She speaks slowly and gently with insights that help me make meaningful con-nections. Our conversations create a sanctuary for me to unfold and explore what arises for me.

Through Somatic Experiencing, a body-centered therapy, I am learning how to speak about past trauma while staying present. I am honoring and naming physical sensations and allowing the wisdom of my body to guide our sessions.

Kristin teaches me how to stay grounded in the present moment to keep myself from falling into what she calls "the trauma vortex." That dark hole used to swallow me when I was triggered or on the edge of flashbacks and intrusive memories.

Through our work together, she instructs me about "pendulation," a Somatic Experiencing technique that helps the nervous system begin to feel safer by touching the past and then returning to the present before there is emotional flooding.

"When we are working with traumatic memories, we need to dip one toe in the water, instead of diving in completely and being flooded," Kristin explains.

I know what it is like to swing between dissociation and a deluge of painful memories.

Disconnecting from reality makes me vulnerable to re-creating the past in the present, because I am not living from a place of integration. This internal split also keeps me from fully knowing who I am and what I desire. I lose access not only to my pain but also to my joy and connection to life. I can feel invulnerable for a while, but the cost is severe. It makes me feel alone, unknown, and hollow.

Flooding, although filled with emotional truth, incapacitates me and makes me feel trapped inside a relentless cycle of abuse. Flooding keeps me feeling like a perpetual victim, as if what happened in the past is always happening and always *will* happen.

Dissociation—splitting off from my experiences—helped me to survive. It was a form of self-protection. Yet self-protection becomes self-abandonment when we don't learn how to come home to our own bodies. Our soul healing requires a return to the body. A home-coming to the present moment, a way of holding space for all our experiences, all our parts to be witnessed.

I felt trapped by my body, as if being embodied was the cause of my suffering. Yet through this reclamation of my body, I am coming to know the richness of my own soul.

Learning the art of pendulation and other mindfulness techniques through Somatic Experiencing gives me another way to relate to the trauma that is still impacting my nervous system and my body's abil-ity to feel safe in the world. Instead of swinging violently between dissociation and flooding, I can gently move between my wise body in the present and the images and emotions of memories.

Listening to the language of my body with expert guidance helps me find my center, my core awareness. My body offers my path to integration because no matter how my times my psyche split off to survive, all the traumatic events happened to *one* body. *My* body.

I can touch my own skin and say, *"Mine."* So many men tried to tell me my body was theirs or belonged to their deity. My mind split off to survive that devastation. But I can call every part of me back home through Somatic Experiencing, because there is finally a safe home to come back to.

During one of our sessions, I confide in Kristin, "I feel like my body is something I just drag around with me. I have to take it places, but it's not really me. It doesn't feel safe to be in my body."

Another time, while we are discussing some of my memories of being physically restrained when I was trafficked, I tell her, "I don't want to be here right now. I feel like I want to get up and run away."

"Where would you like to go?" Kristin asks.

"Outside. I feel trapped."

"We can go outside," she responds.

I am so relieved. We walk to a park across the street, moving side by side in silence. As we walk together, I feel the tightness in my chest soften. My breath deepens and my mind relaxes. My feet connect with the earth.

Her intuition to let my body move is far more healing for me than endlessly dissecting why I feel trapped. Kristin doesn't try to persuade me that I am safe now. She realizes I need to express the energy arising in this moment.

In other sessions, I notice specific gestures my body wants to express. The two most common gestures involve self-protection. A simple movement of my arms pushing someone away to create space and boundaries. It comes up when I am recounting experiences of rape or abuse, as well experiences in my dating life when I felt disrespected by men.

The other gesture is pulling my knees up to my chest and wrapping my arms around them with my head tilted down, so I am in a tight egg shape. When I talk about my head injuries, I cover my head with my hands, which gives me a sense of comfort and safety.

Kristin teaches me to trust what my body wants to express without having to understand why I had that instinct or what it meant. But as I give myself permission to move in ways that feel self-protective and soothing, images and words usually surface to give me a sense of the significance. Sometimes the images are parts of a memory or a symbolic representation of a specific memory.

Other times, the images are more mythic or archetypal. Multiple experiences can be combined in one scene. As I am speaking and working with gestures, I can see a scene with multiple perpetrators from childhood to the present day. It isn't a memory as much as a mythical container for emotional memory that helps me integrate many experiences. Working with the imagery along with my body to tell the story gives me a more unified approach for what previously felt fractured.

The first scene that comes to me during our therapy sessions is set in a dark forest. In this inner vision, the forest is my sacred place, yet I have been hunted there by a pack of black wolves with yellow eyes. They surround my naked body, feeding off of me, ripping the flesh from my body, particularly around the chest and stomach.

Each of the wolves is a man who raped me, abused me, or made me feel worthless. It is not just an assault on me, but on the Sacred Feminine.

I am gradually moving away from seeing my life as torn, ripped into fragments of poetry, shreds of some original ancient text I cannot decipher. The fragments feel true, but they never quite fit in a way that makes sense of my life. Too much is missing: the connective tissue, the transitions, the context and luminous ligaments that would hold it all together.

THERAPY CENTERED ON Somatic Experiencing enables me to craft a story that includes all of me: all of my images, sensations, gestures, and instincts. I call this my Story DNA.

I envision my Story DNA as a double helix of pleasure and pain. One strand of the double helix is the time line of my trauma. The other strand is the time line of my joy. Integration through narrative is the core of my healing, and this integration unfolds through a storytelling process that honors the wisdom of my body as the unifying force.

In sessions with Kristin, when I am focusing on a painful sensation in my body, she says, "Notice that and now notice a part of your body that doesn't feel that way. Is there a part that is not in pain?" I scan my body and notice where I am calm or relaxed. This contrast, this counterpoint, helps me remember that I can shift my attention and witness my wholeness.

I am not one point of pain my mind fixates on. I am a whole woman, a compassionate witness, a mothering presence who can descend and ascend. Together I rest with Persephone in an open field and see the dance of our double helix, our Story DNA, one constellation in a vast sky.

I take the hand of the Sacred Child within and say,

"I have been waiting for you. It is safe to come home now. I have prepared a secure place for you, in my own body, my own sacred female flesh, wild blood, and dancing bones. I am moonstone skin. I am carnelian womb. I am turquoise skeleton. I am the grove of the goddess, and there will be no more trespassing."

chapter nine

Descending with Inanna

I am the priestess of untamed light.

IN THE PAST, AS I TRIED to escape my flesh and split off from my
trauma, it created more suffering. Although dissociation helped
me survive, it also kept me from knowing the truth of my own
desires.

Before I received effective help through trauma therapy, making decisions was extremely difficult. I didn't know who, or what,
I could trust. I was so accustomed to having other people mediate
reality for me. My trauma cut me off from what I needed most to
heal: my own embodied wisdom and soul voice.

Disconnected from the wisdom of my body, silencing her messages with religious doctrines, addictions, and the elusive search for
love outside of myself, I lost touch with what I truly wanted as a
woman. Body-centered therapies restored me to my primal instincts,
the fierce knowing I had abandoned trying to survive my abuse.

Who can tell me what I want? Who can tell me who I am apart
from all the false scripts I inherited? How can I discern my own
inner voice of love from the alluring voices of others promising an-
swers and absolute certainty? How can I live the mystery of my life

with reverence and joy without turning to someone else's architecture, their blueprint for living?

Through my recovery, I am learning that all the knowledge I crave can only be uncovered by reclaiming my desire as sacred. I sense an intuitive, feminine knowledge beneath all the claims of absolute truth and the official historical record of men's philosophies.

In my teens and twenties, I went searching for this in literature, art, music, and books. After working with Kristin, I am able to locate this uncensored knowing in the language of my own body. My body was always speaking, but I learned early in life not to listen.

My body is honest when I struggle to be. She keeps saying, "There is nothing wrong with me. There is something wrong with what happened to me. Century after century, there is something wrong with the way we have been devalued, raped, enslaved, burned at the stake. I am not broken. They are. They cannot break the law of love. They break themselves by what they do."

Through careful study and reflection, I see my story is connected to a greater story of women's voices being silenced and buried. Making this connection helps me uncover two core emotions I have banished into the darkness: desire and rage. Desire and rage were not safe for me to feel unless they were channeled into helping others.

The violation of other women and girls made me angry. But when I thought about my own trafficker, the anger did not come. Eventually, healthy outrage returned to me after I honestly explored desire. It was impossible for me to fully feel and take ownership of my anger, when I was not honoring my desires or witnessing how they had been violated.

Now I begin to write out my desires, from small gifts and nurturing experiences to decadent dreams and adventures. I curate my list and give myself permission to fulfill at least one of these desires each week. Most of these desires are simple luxuries. Others require more planning.

My daily ritual of writing down my desires by hand in a beautiful journal gives me permission to make my own pleasure a priority. One of those desires, which I have held in my heart since I was a little girl, taking French lessons at school, is to visit Paris.

I can always find a reason I should not travel to France: the expense, the time away from my commitments, the creeping sense that it is a romantic cliché and a bit overdone for a lost American girl to find herself in Paris. Yet Paris, ever the insistent seductress, keeps calling to me. I know the art galleries alone would be worth the trip. And I have such fond memories of the language, which I learned soon after my escape from trafficking. The sound of the French accent soothed me as a child.

Anaïs Nin and Collette, Simone de Beauvoir and Hélène Cixous, all the luminaries of Gertrude Stein's circle in the Left Bank, captured my imagination as a young writer. I read Rimbaud and Baudelaire as a teen, drawn to the raw sensuality of their work. The rich legacy of art in Paris finally persuades me to go and wander her streets.

On my way to Paris, I stop in an airport café for my connecting flight and order a glass of pinot noir. As I sip my wine and write in my journal, I see an image of my grandmother. It is as if Grammy suddenly appears in the seat in front of me to join me for a drink on my way to France.

She brings a message of only one word: *"Repass,"* she says and disappears. Repass is her maiden name, derived from the original

French, which has several possible meanings. The meaning I translate from her visitation is "return."

"What are you telling me to return to, Grammy?" I wonder.

I do not receive a reply. I write down her message in my journal and finish my wine. I wonder if it is connected to our French ancestors. Why is she appearing to me now? I always felt connected to her spirit after her passing, but this is different. She shows up in a vision to share a message over red wine, then vanishes. Evidently, she still has a flair for the dramatic in the afterlife.

When I arrive, I map out my trip with all the museums and galleries I want to visit and allow space to improvise in between. Just like many of her visitors, I admire the architecture of Paris, her exquisitely tended gardens, towering sculptures, and cobblestone streets, the artful way shopkeepers create and display their offerings.

I first notice the attention to beauty and detail. Delicate chocolates, vintage books, elegant lingerie, glistening perfume bottles, a pyramid of immaculate pastel macaroons, the pour of the wine at an intimate café—all the small gestures that flirt with the senses remind me to return to the daily pleasures of living.

But this is not the return my grandmother calls me to embrace. I can sense something older and deeper than what I see in the surface beauty of the City of Lights.

I am delighted by Paris and deeply lonely. Although I have friends I can reach out to, I mostly stay in solitude during my trip. This loneliness runs deeper than desiring companionship. It is a soul hunger similar to the one I often felt as I wandered the streets of downtown Austin late at night.

I am seeking something I cannot name.

I am grateful for what is unfolding in my life. I am gifted with an empathetic, wise therapist and beginning to explore and honor my desires. My career as a writer, speaker, and human rights activist is growing. Yet something's missing. I am missing some part of me.

One evening at sunset, I wander for so long I don't know where I am or how to navigate my way back to the apartment I rented. My cell phone has died, and I don't have a map. My useless phone contains the address of my rental, so I can't tell a cab driver where to take me.

As l look around, I spot a small church and walk inside. Nothing in the iconography of the empty sanctuary resonates with me, but I feel drawn to go behind the main room, down a winding hallway. Tucked away behind the altar lies a statue of Saint Teresa of Avila, the Christian poet and mystic.

When I see her, I start to weep unexpectedly. I think of her passionate communion with God. She wrote about her life of devotion, "All that is needed is the will to love," and she beautifully defined prayer as "being on terms of friendship with God."

I miss this part of myself. The part of me who adored the compassionate Christ I encountered as a child, the incarnation of God my abusers did not see or understand in spite of their claims to the Christian religion.

As I cry, I pray aloud, "Do not let him take you from me. Do not let him take you from me. You know my heart. Do not let him take you from me."

Without thinking, I am pouring out my pain, beside a hidden statue of a woman whose life was defined by her lavish love and devotion to the Divine.

This is *not* what I expected from Paris.

This is not the Paris of designer clothes, underground dance clubs, and champagne toasts. This is not the sexy sophistication I hear my friends coo about.

Yet in this moment, I feel held and heard. In a narrow hall with dim lights, I pray for complete union with Divine Love without the interference of my trafficker and all the men who abused me in God's name.

A gentle voice inside me says, *"He does not speak for me. They do not speak for me."* Hearing this inner wisdom gives me peace. It makes me feel I can receive the revelation of love directly.

I never have to listen to another person who claims to speak for God. I can listen to the voice of love within me. Whether that voice feels feminine or masculine does not matter. What matters is that I can trust my own connection to love, unconditional love.

I imagined Paris would be a decadent immersion into culinary delights, fascinating shows, and art. On the surface, it proves to be all of that for me. I see a sultry burlesque performance at the Crazy Horse and feast with two French friends at a lovely café, talking for hours about feminist activism, theater, French philosophy, and creative writing.

I fall in love with the Rodin sculpture garden and the Salvador Dalí museum in Montmartre. I enjoy the flirtatious French men, charming boutiques, and smell of fresh bread in each arrondissement.

I appreciate the regal sensuality of the city. But my encounter with Paris is not light and romantic at the core. I feel like I have been here before and I am back to reclaim a part of myself I have lost, a memory of my soul. Grammy's message reverberates inside me, *"Repass. Repass. Repass."*

When I enter the Cathedral of Notre-Dame, I feel drawn to the right side of the building, where I discover a statue of Joan of Arc.

The plaque beside her explains she was burned at the stake for being a heretic. "Of course they burned you," I muse. "And now they claim you as their saint." I light a candle at the altar, knowing that I, too, was thrown to the fire in this lifetime, labeled a heretic, a dangerous woman, unworthy of life.

I wonder, "How many of us have been called unholy simply because we are passionate and powerful? How many of us have been damned, demeaned, and discarded for sharing our truth? What if after all these centuries we become the fire we once feared?"

One Paris offers me rich hot chocolate at Angeline's and the sleek seductions of the burlesque dancers. She gives me sensual photography, labyrinthine strolls, and tendrils of cigarette smoke curling around melancholy gazes. She shows me her allure.

Yet another story beneath this story calls to me: a legacy of burning.

The legacy of women like Joan of Arc and medieval mystic Marguerite Porete, who wrote a treatise on the unconditional love of God. These women hungered for God and shared their mystic visions with the world. But they were sentenced to death by fire for simply being women and speaking their spiritual truth.

I did not intend for my trip to Paris to be a spiritual pilgrimage. I traveled to France to honor a childhood desire and explore her many pleasures. I did not know I would be drawn into a deeper story, the story of a woman who has become fire, so she no longer fears the flame. I was led into the legacy of burning with Joan of Arc and can say, as she once did, "I am not afraid. I was born to do this."

RELINQUISHING THE FEAR of my own wild and worthy nature, I am reborn and remember:

You cannot burn me, I am fire.
You cannot drown me, I am the flood.
You cannot bury me, I am the landslide.

When you force me down, I rise above.
You cannot separate me from the love I am.
My origin and destination.
I am the priestess
of untamed light.

After I return from my trip to Paris, visionary filmmaker Deborah Kampmeier asks me to act in her film *Split*, a surrealistic journey based on the ancient Sumerian myth of Inanna. In the film, a young, aspiring actress is forced to confront all the parts of herself she has disowned: her rage, her truth, her authentic sexuality, and her power.

Through the course of an emotionally abusive relationship and the demands of acting in a play based on the text "Descent of Inanna," she wrestles with what it means to come into her voice and live with personal sovereignty as a woman.

I play a small part in the ensemble. My character, an actor and survivor of child sex trafficking, shares part of her story in a healing circle. The day we shoot the scene, I relax on a blanket on the bare floor of the old Domino Sugar factory in Brooklyn. I listen to Florence and the Machine's "Seven Devils" on repeat, read poetry, and write in my journal as we wait for our time on set.

I am surrounded by a fierce group of women, many half-naked and painted with spirals for our ensemble scenes where we dance with masks. When we come into a circle for the scene Deborah calls

"I Speak," it does not feel as if we are acting. Although we are given a script, the emotional truth of each confession carries the real pain of our experiences of violence, the ways we have been silenced and shamed.

The scene opens as the theater director says, "What have you silenced? What have you buried away and hidden in the dark?" One by one, each woman enters into character and shares her story of abuse: domestic violence, rape, incest, genital mutilation, and sexual shaming.

When the camera moves to me, I am already crying in response to each woman's performance. I share my lines about sex trafficking from a place of primal truth, tears flooding my face as I rock back and forth. In the moment, consumed with grief, I shout, "I was seven!"

I did not plan to say this.

It erupts from my body as if I had been waiting all my life for this moment to mourn with my sisters. In the final edit of the film, many of the "I Speak" lines are cut, including some of mine. But my raw confession is still there: I was *seven*.

"The Descent of Inanna," written by Sumerian priestess Enheduanna, is part of a series of hymns and stories illuminating the worldview and devotional practices of ancient Sumer. According to several scholars, Enheduanna may be the first published author in human history.

After reading Deborah's provocative script, I want to study translations of the original texts. Through this exploration, I discover powerful healing insights for women and what it takes for us to finally become whole. It is the path of the priestess.

The story begins with two sisters, Inanna, Queen of Heaven and Earth, and Ereshkigal, Queen of the Underworld. Inanna decides to descend to the underworld to be with her sister, Ereshkigal, while she mourns the loss of her husband.

In order to descend to the underworld, Inanna must pass through seven gates. At each gate, she is required to give up something she is wearing until she arrives at the final gate and must surrender her robe. When she questions why she must surrender her belongings at each stop, she is told, "The ways of the underworld are perfect."

After hearing this seven times, Inanna enters her sister's throne room, completely naked, stripped of all her jewelry and clothing. Instead of welcoming her sister, Ereshkigal "fastens on Inanna the eye of death," strikes her, and hangs her from a meat hook to rot. Let's just say Ereshkigal has some serious rage.

When Inanna's friend Ninshubur doesn't see her come back from her underworld visit after three days, she cries out to several father gods to help her bring Inanna safely home. The first two, Father Enil and Father Nanna, are not keen on helping out. They basically say, "She can rot in hell." Fortunately, the third one, Father Enki, is moved by Ninshubur's plea. He loves Inanna and decides to intervene by creating two new creatures from the dirt under his fingernails.

These creatures are neither male nor female and small enough to fly through the cracks of the underworld gates. Father Enki sends them with specific instructions to mirror back to Ereshkigal everything she expresses, to hear her cries and show her compassion. These magical creatures reach her throne room, and every time she moans in pain, they echo her:

"Oh! Oh! My insides!" she cries.

"Oh! Oh! Your insides!" they cry.

After several rounds of mourning with her, and naming the places where it hurts (her belly, her back, her heart, her liver), she stops and looks at the creatures and says, "Who are you, moaning, groaning, and sighing with me?" She wants to know who is showing her this empathy, so she can give them a gift. They turn down her offer to give them "the river in its fullness" and "the fields in harvest."

"Speak then! What do you wish?" she shouts.

"We wish only the corpse that hangs from the hook on the wall," they reply.

So Ereshkigal lets them have Inanna's corpse. They sprinkle her body with magical substances and bring her back to life.

The myth continues, but this is the heart of the story: Inanna's descent through the seven gates, her murder by the enraged Ereshkigal, and the compassionate witnesses that heal the Queen of the Underworld, so Inanna can rise again.

What most fascinates me when I read the text is that the turning point of the story revolves around two creatures who have empathy for the sister who lives in the shadows, the one who is filled with rage and grief, hidden underground, banished to the darkness. She embodies all the attributes women are trained to disown. She is our collective shadow.

After exploring Paris and uncovering a deeper story, I am open to where the myth of Inanna might lead me. I *thought* I was acting in a film to contribute my voice to a script I believed in. But that was only the surface. On a soul level, it was an invitation to descend with intention, to face my shadow self, my furious and formidable sister.

I begin by imagining what Ereshkigal might want to say to her sister, Queen of Heaven and Earth, her sister who was favored and lived in the light. What lessons does she have to teach Inanna? What forbidden wisdom does she carry? I write a song in her voice as a way of entering into her perspective. I ask myself, "Why is she hurting? Why is she so angry?"

When I studied creative writing at Naropa University, Anne Waldman taught our class about the concept of "investigative poetics," which is essentially a way of approaching poetry as a process of investigation and inquiry.

When I want to know something from the inside out, I write.

So I create a piece called "Song for Inanna," in which Ereshkigal's voice can finally be heard.

The ways of the underworld are perfect.
The ways of the underworld are wise.
Let me take you deep below the surface
to secrets you have banished from the light.

I know all the ways that they cut you.
I know they stripped you of your choice.
I am the radiant darkness
calling you to reclaim your voice.

They will divide and conquer
if you turn away from me.
I am the one you must uncover
if you want to set your fire free.

I hold your shame and your anger.
I hold your pain and your grief,

but I also hold your power,
Come and join me underneath.

There can be no resurrection
unless you are willing to descend
How can we be sisters
when you won't listen to where I've been?

The ways of the underworld are perfect.
Do not question this descent.
Honor the ways you survived,
how you fractured and you split.

Do you see the ways that they cut her?
How the little ones are sold?
Do you see the girls you've forgotten
dancing in your kingdom of gold?

This ancient Sumerian myth, written by a priestess, holds a powerful message for women who feel divided and split off from their core. The story illuminates the inner violence and soul loss that occur when we ignore our shadow side, the places of raw pain, shame, and fury.

I don't feel compelled to act on every emotion I feel, but in order to feel whole, I need to bear witness to what has been hidden in darkness, the parts of my psyche that are waiting to be heard, to be seen, to be loved. The parts I conceal. The parts I force underground because I believe they are unacceptable.

At first glance, Ereshkigal is not a lovable character. She is angry, murderous, and unmerciful. This sister has *issues*. Yet when she is met with tenderness, mirrored by two creatures whose only mission is to fully witness her, she sets in motion a resurrection. She lets Inanna off the hook because she finally receives the gift of empathy. They are no longer at war.

I didn't relate to Ereshkigal when I read the story the first few times. She's a bit too homicidal for me. She never listens to her sister or finds out why she came. She forces Inanna to strip on her way down and then immediately fixes a death eye on her without even a brief "Hello." These are not attractive qualities. But after I act in the film and write the song, I can *feel* this part of my psyche and *see* this in other women.

Exploring the energy of Ereshkigal and witnessing her character in the film challenge me to be more honest about where I am still hiding, still playing a role, even if that role appears to be good and brave. Ereshkigal is not interested in making us look appealing.

In fact, she is an archetype of the wise, wild woman that patriarchal cultures teach us to fear. She does not act like a lady. She is unleashed and untamed, manic and messy. She turns hideous when she is not heard.

My anger wants a witness. My anger not only flows from my personal story. It flows underground like volcanic lava from an ancestral story, the stories of every woman in my maternal line who experienced violence, exploitation, and abuse. The fire builds inside me from centuries past, and this collective energy wants to erupt.

I am comfortable with my tears. Tears feel tender and feminine. But I need to make peace with the howling, raging Underworld Queen inside of me. The one who never forgets the ways she has been devalued and cast aside.

I start to see why Ereshkigal wanted to destroy her sister. Inanna is everything patriarchal cultures love. She is pleasing, beautiful, and light, adored by gods and men. She does not trouble others with her pain, her rage, her truth. And her sister could not stand it.

The Ereshkigal part of me is easy to reject and project onto someone else, yet she holds powerful medicine. Meeting the exiled sister inside myself prepared the way for a deeper experience of sisterhood in the world. In an old sugar factory in Brooklyn, I dance with my shadow and hear her howling.

Now when she says, "Oh, Oh! My insides!"

I say, "Girl, your insides!"

And when she says, "Oh! Oh! My heart!"

I say, "Oh! Oh! Your heart! I am *listening*."

This core wisdom helps me heal. By holding every part of my being with relentless empathy, I am finding freedom.

PART TWO

The Art of Survivorship

chapter ten

Untamed Light

How Survivors Become Leaders

We are the untamed.
We are the unashamed.
We are beautiful justice.
Just watch us rise.

Although I am deeply intimate with the cost of being devalued on the basis of my gender, this is an issue that is far greater than my personal story. My experience with sex trafficking, sexual assault, and domestic violence is simply an entry point into an important and urgent conversation about the way women and girls are treated around the world.

In the United States, one out of every six women will be sexually assaulted. Forty-five percent of those women are assaulted before the age of eighteen. One out of every four women will experience some form of domestic violence, and the greatest predictor for experiencing domestic violence is childhood sexual assault.

Although most girls will never experience sex trafficking, it is far more prevalent than previously acknowledged. A recent study by the University of Texas estimated that seventy-nine thousand children are currently being trafficked in Texas. The vast majority of these victims are girls.

Though many will escape the ravages of physical violence, they still must face their own challenges within the continuum of misogyny and sexism. Women experience sexual harassment in the workplace, online, and on the streets. Many still encounter pay inequality and the virulent attacks waged against female leaders in media and politics. In the United States, we still have not elected a woman as president or even ratified the Equal Rights Amendment, the proposed legislation that would finally guarantee equal rights for women in our Constitution.

Every day we are flooded with countless examples of women and girls being devalued. Gender violence is simply one part of a continuum of cultural and political practices that negate our worth. Selling human beings into sex trafficking is the ultimate conclusion of an ideology that defines us as sexual commodities.

Human trafficking is an extreme form of exploitation, but dehumanization occurs across a spectrum of experiences that both normalize and reinforce this violence. The heart of my work is not to merely advocate for an end to gender violence, but to understand and heal the personal and cultural wounds that teach us we are less than human.

This healing begins with me. The foundation of my recovery has been a fierce commitment to my own liberation. Living the truth of who I am is freedom. In my recovery, I learned I have the power to choose who I want to be in the world.

The men who abused me do not define me. I am not defined by the way others try to name me. My identity flows from this spiritual truth: I am loved, and love has given me the gift of choice. I am an alchemist, transmuting pain into the power of compassion.

COURAGE IS CONTAGIOUS

From the streets to the workplace, sexual harassment is the background noise of many of our lives. Sometimes we don't speak out because we are frightened or humiliated. Other times, we remain silent because it is so achingly common and we have learned this is simply the way the world works.

As brave testimonies poured out from women who said they were harassed and assaulted by producer Harvey Weinstein, I witnessed each woman taking back her power. When a survivor speaks her truth, countless more will decide the time has come to speak her own.

Courage is contagious. I know, because the most difficult decision I ever made was to tell the truth about my life.

In the beginning, I confided in others to heal my own body and soul. My experiences are not who I am, but I share this truth because speaking out saved my life.

Eventually, I spoke about my experiences in public spaces because I wanted to create my own path to emotional justice and encourage others in their healing. Abuse impacts approximately one in three women around the world; violence should not be the cost of being female on this earth.

I still talk about my experiences because I want to encourage those who experience any form of abuse to tell the truth that will set them free. As individuals, we are strong and resilient. As a collective, we are a force to be reckoned with.

I give voice to my past because I believe in the unconditional worth of women and girls. I believe we should never have to carry our pain in isolation or live with the fear and shame that abusers leave behind in our hearts and minds when they are finished with our bodies.

Not everyone wants to hear our truths; not everyone will stand up and celebrate our resilience and bravery. But the choice to share your experience, on your terms, when you are ready, is a form of creative power that can never be taken from you.

We are not victims, or even merely survivors. We are the new generation of leaders, fiercely devoted to creating a world where our lives are valued. And that begins with valuing our own voices.

NOTHING CAN STEAL YOUR BEAUTY

We have all been lied to about who we are. Through trauma, re-lationships, and media, we have been taught that we are not good enough. We are bombarded by the message that we are separated from the love we crave and seduced into believing that if we strive harder, accomplish more, give more, perform our roles, buy new products, follow new gurus, or subject ourselves to another diet or self-help program, we will finally arrive.

But the glimpses of joy and peace do not last because they are built on the underlying fallacy that we have to *earn* love and *prove* our worth by changing our external circumstances.

You may be in pain right now. You may feel disconnected from the truth of your unconditional worth. But nothing can take away your value.

There is nothing you can do to make God love you any less. And there is nothing you can do to make God love you any more. This is the way of wild grace. It is safe to rest here.

No matter what you have experienced, you cannot render yourself unworthy. You are a child of the Divine. Your essence is eternal. The war that has been waged against your body, mind, and soul through abuse does not alter who you are.

This is what I understand about abuse. Abuse, whether physical or verbal, tells you lies about who you are. The more abuse you have experienced, the more deceptions you have to illuminate and release, so you can return to your core truth.

Coming into agreement with false stories helped us survive devastating trauma and loss. It diminished the pain for a while, and let us feel we had some control over a situation in which we were being hurt. If I am attacked over and over again and I can't stop it, it helps me survive to finally accept, "This is who I am. This is what I deserve. This is what is possible for me. This is just the way life is."

If I don't, then every time I am verbally or physically abused, I have to feel the pain of wanting something I believe I cannot have. So, holding on to false stories may make us feel safer for a while because it helps to numb the pain.

But eventually, these stories no longer serve us. They even make us vulnerable to being harmed in a similar way in the future because we unconsciously seek someone to confirm the lies we had to cling to in order to survive.

PRAYER FOR SELF-COMPASSION

In a recovery group for survivors of child sex trafficking in Texas, I talked to teen girls about the power of self-compassion and how essential it is for our recovery.

"You can look at self-esteem as when you see yourself as having value and self-compassion as treating yourself with kindness. Our sense of value may change from day to day depending on what we derive our value from: how we look, who is paying attention to us, what we accomplish.

"If we have a spiritual point of view on our value, it may be more consistent. But no matter what is happening, we can choose to be kind and gentle with ourselves. Self-compassion is both a choice and a process. What are some healthy ways you comfort yourself when you are hurting?"

"Listening to music," said one shy girl, gazing down.

"Yeah, listening to music," echoed another.

"Drawing."

"Writing in my journal."

"Spending time with the horses. I want to spend more time with the horses."

A fifteen-year-old curvy Caucasian girl with thick glasses, her brown hair in a pixie cut, grew irritated. "Why should I be kind to myself? It's my fault," she exclaimed stubbornly.

"What's your fault?"

"Being a *prostitute*," she yelled. "I was a *prostitute*," she shouted again. "I wanted the drugs."

I paused. Looking around the room, I could see the other girls were upset. Many of them had worked very hard to stop blaming themselves for being abused and exploited.

"It's not your fault," another girl yelled back, as if begging her to stop the tirade.

I knew if I pushed back, it would only make her more defensive. So I said, "I'm not going to take your story away from you. Sometimes our stories help us survive, but we can let them go when we don't need them anymore. How old were you the first time someone forced you to do something sexual that you didn't want to do?"

"Eight. It was my father and grandfather."

"So you learned that was who you were and why you were here."

"Yeah," she confessed, softening a little.

"Who would you be without that story? What would you have to feel?"

"Oh . . . you're *good* . . . ," she said, staring intently.

She studied me with her arms across her chest, now more curious than angry. "Okay. How do I do it? How do I have self-compassion?" she demanded bluntly.

"What is something that comforts you and helps you feel connected to love?" I asked.

"I like to pray. I have a prayer closet. I turned the closet in my bedroom into a prayer closet, and I go there to talk to God."

"Wonderful. Would you be open to praying for God to help you love yourself the way God loves you?"

"Yeah. I can do that," she responded.

"Good. Do you want to write a prayer now that you can hang in your closet?"

"Yeah," she said eagerly. "And then I can read it *every day*," she shared, excited by the possibility.

She immediately started writing out her prayer on a piece of notebook paper, moving her hand quickly across the page.

I turned to speak to the whole group. "Treating ourselves with kindness is a choice we can make every day. It is also a process. As we make that choice, we learn more and more what it means to love who we are. And our community can help us when we forget."

She looked up at me and smiled. "Can I show you my prayer closet now?" she asked.

YOUR SOUL SONG

Nothing can separate you from Divine Love. Love is who you are. It is where you come from and where you are going. All our steps in recovery are a remembrance of this truth. Whether you return to the birthright of your worth through trauma therapy, healing community, bodywork, mindful movement, creative expression, immersion in nature, or spiritual practices, such as prayer, meditation, or seeking solace in sacred texts, your soul knows the way home.

Listen to her wisdom. Listen to the quiet, yet powerful, voice within you that knows what you need to heal, and remember you have always been sacred.

I am not here to tell you what this path of remembrance should look like. Your exquisite soul voice has her own songs to sing, her own path of unfolding. I have seen that when women choose to devote their lives to a way of healing and liberation above all else, they uncover the medicine they seek, and this soul medicine ultimately becomes a sacred gift to the communities they love.

The lies that have been forced on me and anchored with violence have been relentless. My healing and liberation have been a path of releasing the agreements and stories that caused me suffering, so I can rest in the truth of my worth.

There is a new generation of women leaders rising without shame or apology. We are courageously telling our stories and relinquishing the false narratives we have been told about who we are. We are bringing everything into the light.

What previous generations covered over, silenced, or trivialized as "women's issues," we are bringing into the epicenter of politics and culture. The generations before us prepared the way with their passion and wisdom. Now it is our time.

SURVIVORSHIP

There is an essential transition of identity for many of the women and girls I mentor. When we first meet, they are often just beginning to speak about their experiences of abuse and exploitation. Some are so entrenched in self-blame, they don't yet recognize their own victimization. Yet I see each survivor as a potential leader.

Through compassionate community, we begin to see that it is safe to give voice to our truth and be honest about how we have been hurt. This transition out of denial and into the raw reality of our lives creates an opportunity for us to begin taking back our power and becoming survivors.

We learn to love who we are by learning to love our truth, no matter how painful it may be. This prepares the way for us to envision another possibility. There is room for the mystic, the misfit, the outsider, the ones who never found their way home.

As we process and integrate our trauma, we gain access to our core desires, to the parts of our soul that have been split off, silenced, or rejected. We remember or awaken to dreams that reveal who we are and why we are here.

A survivor becomes a leader when she honors her desires, embraces all her experiences, and expresses her unique gifts to create change in the world. She is no longer at war within, so she can be a warrior for peace. She steps into the role of priestess, healer, and guide.

This is the way of survivorship. I see survivorship as the process of self-definition and reclamation that allows those who have experienced abuse to live with dignity. Abuse tells us lies about who we are. Abuse tells us we are worthless, powerless, alone. Abuse teaches us that our voices and desires do not matter.

So, survivorship, or what I call Survivor Leadership, is essentially a return to the truth of who we are and the undeniable value of our own voices. It is the transition from the trauma of victimization to personal sovereignty over our bodies and lives, as we become catalysts for change.

I learned this path of transformation in community with my survivor sisters. Before I learned how to have compassion for myself, I had compassion for the women I joined in healing circles. When I was still caught in shame and self-blame, I felt deep empathy for them. I felt protective of them and could not fathom how anyone could feel entitled to harm them. I saw their resilience, their light, their loving hearts.

As I witnessed this, I began to imagine what it would be like to treat myself with the same fierce, protective love I felt for my sisters. I started to ask, "Am I willing to give myself what I desire most for them? Am I willing to embody in my own life what I hope for my sisters?"

I experimented and explored. "What would it look like to value myself today? What do I truly desire? Am I willing to honor this?"

WISDOM OF DESIRE

Ella was fifteen when the Austin Police Department referred her to me for mentoring. When we connected at a downtown coffee shop, the striking, thin African American girl struggled to look directly into my eyes. Ella had already survived years of drug abuse, including an addiction to meth. She spoke softly and kept her head down while she sipped her coffee.

I didn't ask her about her past. I knew she would speak about her experience of trafficking when she was ready. Instead, we talked about her dreams for the future.

"What do you want to focus on?" I asked.

"I want to write a book about my life," Ella said. "People need to know that stuff like this happens to girls as young as me."

"You will write a powerful book and transform lives," I said. "I'm writing a book, too. Do you want to start meeting up to work on our writing together?"

She nodded.

As we left the coffee shop and walked around Lady Bird Lake, Ella told me about her family and what happened when she was "selling herself." A handsome older man she met outside of a restaurant offered to let her stay with him after she ran away from a drug-treatment facility in Dallas. She thought he cared about her, but he forced her into prostitution to "pay the rent."

Ella told me it was her choice.

I asked her, "What would happen if you didn't work?"

"He would beat me," she responded.

"No one should ever hit you. You did what you had to do to survive. It's not your fault."

Ella looked down at the trail. "Yeah. I didn't want to do that."

"Also, you were underage. It is illegal for those adult men to be with you," I reminded her.

"Yeah," she said.

I met with Ella often for coffee over the next couple of years. We usually chatted about her latest boyfriend. She always told me how amazing these men were, and I asked the same questions, so I could support her in protecting herself.

"How old is he?

How does he treat you?

What drugs is he on?

Is he employed?

Has he been to prison?

Does he have kids?

Does he pay child support?

What are his tattoos?

Remember, girl, no face tattoos. Okay? That is an indication he *does not* make good life choices."

Ella would laugh as she answered me.

"They should treat you like a queen," I reminded her.

"I know," she would reply.

We always set aside time to write. Ella created poetry in her journal with passionate focus. Then she would shyly slide her poems across the table for me to read as soon as she finished. After reading each one, I would tell her what resonated with me and encourage her to continue. Most often I said, "This is powerful." Her uncensored truth was breathtaking.

Ella started to see herself as a writer. I met with her not only to support her writing her poetry collection, but to give her the opportunity to define her identity beyond the abuse and exploitation. If she wrote about a part of her past that was too overwhelming, we would take a break and walk together until she felt more grounded.

I took her to poetry readings, one featuring poets performing in solidarity with Black Lives Matter in a small cottage on the East Side. I wanted her to witness black women writers sharing powerful, creative work with a focus on social justice. I wanted Ella to see herself in their stories and imagine who she could become. We went to galleries featuring women's visual art and browsed the young adult sections of bookstores, so she could pick out books that fascinated her.

On her first Survivor Leadership retreat with twelve other trafficking survivors, she shared what she was learning about healing.

I asked the group, "What has helped you most in your recovery?"

When it was Ella's turn to share, she said, "You ask me what I want. No one asks me what I want."

Later that afternoon, when I was driving her to her mom's apartment, she said, "I have something to tell you."

I started to worry. "Is she pregnant? Has she relapsed?"

"Tell me," I said.

"I . . . am . . . *amazing*," she exclaimed.

"Yes, you are. *And* you've been hanging out with me too much," I said, laughing.

I looked over at her, and she held my gaze. She was not ashamed. We both smiled.

"Yes, you are," I repeated.

TRUTH AND LIE

When I hosted a day retreat for teen survivors of sex trafficking in San Antonio, I invited Ella to come with me to help facilitate. She was excited to take the trip and encourage young women who were just starting their recovery.

I opened by sharing my story of overcoming abuse and how I found healing. I told them that knowing their true identity and value is essential for creating what they want in life.

Then I invited them to do an exercise with me called "Truth and Lie." I said, "It is difficult to value yourself when people have told you lies about who you are. I want you to tell me the lies people have told you about who you are. I will start. One lie I was told about who I am is 'You're worthless.' Does anyone want to share a lie they have been told?"

A young woman shouted, "You're only good for sex."

Another girl said, "You're stupid."

One more added, "You'll never amount to anything."

As each one revealed a lie they had been told, the names they had been called, the energy in the room surged and their voices strengthened.

"Now I want you to tell something true about yourself. When has someone told you the truth about who you are?"

They waited quietly.

One girl confessed, "No one has ever told me the truth about who I am."

I could feel the pain of this as she spoke, a constriction in my chest and tightening in my stomach.

"What do *you* know to be true about yourself?" I asked.

"I am brave."

"I am smart," another girl chimed in.

"I am resilient."

As each young woman spoke, I could see a renewed spark in their eyes, their shoulders moving back, heads lifting, chests expanding with more confidence.

"This is why healing community is so important," I said. "Your community will help you remember the truth of who you are and remind you of your worth when you start to forget. You have the power to decide what kind of woman you want to be and the story you will tell about your life. No one can take that from you. No one."

THREE WAYS OF SEEING

One of the gifts of traveling as a speaker and human rights activist is the opportunity to talk with survivors around the world. I have the honor of hearing their stories, seeing their art, laughing over meals, and learning about their passions.

When I visited a shelter for child survivors of sex trafficking in Texas, I hosted a discussion about telling our stories. I offered several creative writing exercises for the girls. In one, we wrote love letters to ourselves, writing out the words we most needed to hear during a time of struggle, and signed our names. Some of the girls offered to read their letters aloud.

The power of their voices filled the room. The staff at the facility fell silent. The girls took a great risk by writing these letters. They allowed themselves to imagine a world where they deserve to be treated with tenderness, a world where they could be comforted when they are in pain, instead of shamed, silenced, and blamed.

I shared with them what I learned from my own process of telling my story. "Your story is not just what happened to you. It is also what you decide you will make it mean. We can't change the past, but we can decide how we will relate to it."

I shared an example from my own life—my brain injury in high school. I said, "I could make the disabilities I had after my head injury mean 'I'm stupid' or 'Bad things always happen to me.' Or I could reframe it as 'I am resilient. I am strong. I have overcome so much.'"

I asked for a volunteer to tell me about a challenge they were facing in their life. A feisty Latina girl with curly hair, who had been slumped down in her chair, blurted out, "Being here!"

"Okay. Being here," I repeated. "Now tell me three different ways you can look at being here."

"Ummm . . . that it sucks and I can't do *anything*."

"What's another way you can look at it?" I continued.

"My life is *over*," she complained dramatically.

"What is one more way? Try to find something positive," I encouraged.

"I can make some new friends."

"Good. What is important about that?" I asked.

She straightened up in her chair. "'Cause we can relate to each other, ya know? We've been through the same things, and we can be like sisters."

"Yes, like sisters. That's why we're here," I said.

BELOVED COMMUNITY

As Martin Luther King Jr. said, "The aftermath of nonviolence is the creation of the beloved community." For me, true community is the key to enduring joy. True community moves beyond a mere collection of people tied by similar interests to the creation of sacred space, where each of us can know ourselves as beloved.

In the end, I find joy in the face of injustice through a return to love: the vast, fierce compassion that includes us all.

It is the great remembering of who we are, our unconditional value and dignity. The restoring of connection when connection has been severed. The war waged against my basic human rights taught me to reverence the power of radical intimacy. This is the kind of relationship that bears luminous witness and shows me I no longer have to carry my pain alone. Intimacy with other survivors helped me transmute my pain into healing wisdom and soul medicine.

There is no greater joy than knowing our worth as human beings. We learn this worth in community when we are heard, respected, and celebrated. A hunger for human rights is a hunger for our voices and our desires to finally matter.

When I face human rights violations in my work as an activist, it is my community that reminds me it is safe to grieve, to have my heart broken open, and, then, to laugh again, to let all the emotions of being human pass through me. Happiness depends on circumstances. Enduring joy is closer to aliveness, a willingness to be with all that is and still sing, because I know love will have the last word.

My path to joy has been a path of self-definition. As poet and activist Audre Lorde said, "If I didn't define myself for myself, I would be crunched into other people's fantasies for me and eaten alive." Abuse taught me that other people's fantasies for me could consume and destroy me. Telling the truth about my life saved me from that erasure.

Here is how I define myself. I am not a victim or even merely a survivor. I am a leader, poet, performing artist, and human rights activist deeply devoted to helping women and girls reclaim their worth. Joy is my birthright and my resistance. I am a woman who has learned my pleasure is sacred, my worth undeniable, and my laughter part of what makes me a force of nature.

When I am in circle with survivors, I do not ask them what they are grieving. I ask them what they are celebrating. We have made our peace and danced with our sorrows. We are not ashamed any longer because the shame was never ours to carry.

My own experience of trauma awakened me to the need for both inner healing and the healing of our planet. I've focused on helping survivors reconnect with their worth, resilience, and creative power. Yet these issues are deeply interconnected with every other challenge we face as a human family.

Ultimately, I see this work as one part of our collective liberation, the restoration of intimacy with ourselves, our communities, the earth, and the sacred in all. We do not have to live in energetic opposition to violence. Radical love is its own resistance. Radical love is not just a reaction. It is the process of creation.

If you are weary of hearing news of devastation and destruction, violence and inequality, exploitation and environmental degradation, I encourage you to return to the revolution of intimacy, the pleasures of community, and the joy that gives you the strength to sing your freedom song. Your soul knows the way.

chapter eleven

Creating Beautiful Justice

What Survivors Deserve

Justice is a mighty wave.
She's coming for the crown you crave.

You think that just because you pay
that all your sins are washed away.

I see you and your crew. You all fall down
as the red light girls rise from the ground.

I MET KHURSHIDA AT A RETREAT FOR survivors of human trafficking hosted by our friend Carissa Phelps. We gathered in a lovely seaside home with more than thirty women to enjoy a weekend in Northern California together.

The house overflowed with laughter and music, delicious food, and soul talk. In the morning, we practiced yoga on a hill overlooking the water. In the afternoons, we surfed and played beach volleyball.

We traded stories on survival and healing. One teen girl had exited trafficking only a few months before joining us. Her pimp beat her so severely she couldn't work for him anymore, so he abandoned her at a hospital.

Others were already established leaders in the movement. There were moments when the younger women needed to slow down, talk, and grieve, but most of the retreat was a time of joy and play on the beach.

When Khurshida and I decided to kayak out into the ocean, I did not know her story. Slowly, she revealed she was trafficked out of India into the United States as a little girl. It was the first time I met a survivor who was trafficked as early as I was.

Most of my survivor friends were trafficked in their teens and early twenties by older men posing as boyfriends. I could relate to their trauma and have compassion for all the abuse they experienced, but their stories were so different from mine.

Meeting another woman who knew what it was like to be exploited as a young child, during a time of such innocence, trust, and vulnerability, helped me feel less alone. By the end of the retreat she called me "sister" and gave me several of her gold bangles to wear. I still treasure her gift.

As little girls, on different sides of the world, we were both being exploited and abused. Yet we not only overcame our trauma, but both found our personal paths to leadership. This is the power of sisterhood.

BROTHELS OF BANGKOK

I was invited to speak at a conference in Bangkok sponsored by the United Nations to address members of Parliament from more than forty Southeast Asian countries. While I was there, I knew I wanted to visit the local red-light district and connect with young women recovering from sexual exploitation.

I was honored to speak to world leaders, passionate men and women, devoted to ending human trafficking and gender violence. I shared how to empower survivors to become leaders, as well as strategies for integrating survivor expertise into policy making.

Legislators from India, Tibet, Japan, and many other countries from the surrounding regions resonated with my message: those who are most impacted by a human rights issue should shape the policies that will directly affect their communities.

As we discussed this essential approach to political change, I knew that a few miles from the luxury hotel where I stayed, teen girls were openly being sold out of brothels. Many of them, born into generational poverty, migrated from rural areas and experienced violence and exploitation after seeking better jobs in the city.

When I walked down one of the main streets of the red-light district with my friend Constance, I witnessed bar after bar filled with white Western men, holding their drinks and checking out the merchandise. Every time I saw a new neon sign advertising girls or heard another wave of men laughing with their crew, I was filled with disgust.

Each one reminded me of my trafficker and the men he sold me to, callous men ruled by their cravings, disconnected from the truth of the suffering they left in their wake. They refused to see what their desires, divorced from the reality of other human lives, ultimately cost.

Although technically it is not legal for the bars in Bangkok to directly sell the girls, they facilitate the transaction and benefit financially. In most of the visible commercial establishments, a buyer picks a girl and then pays the bar an "exit fee" to take her somewhere to perform sexual acts.

To the uneducated eye, it might appear to be consensual. But the histories of abuse, coercion, and poverty tell a different story. There is an illusion of a constant party with copious drinks, loud music, and young smiling girls. Some have numbers pinned to their clingy dresses so they can be quickly identified by a buyer. This ploy conceals the reality of rape, complex trauma, and economic vulnerability. It also hides the fact that many of them are underage.

A few blocks from the bars, a safe house for survivors of sex trafficking shelters girls in their teens and early twenties. Over a beautiful homemade dinner of Thai stews and rice dishes, I spoke to the girls about their experience in recovery.

"What do you love most about being here?" I asked the girls at the dinner table. One of the staff members translated for me. When it was her turn to speak, the shy, slender girl sitting next to me smiled and said, "What I like most about being here is learning about the love of God."

She beamed as she shared this, her face illuminated from within.

"That is beautiful. Thank you for sharing that with me," I replied, in awe of her response. After walking past all the buyers, all the sellers, all the girls still trapped in poverty and exploitation, her answer pierced through my disgust and gave me hope. God was in the redlight district. I saw her in the faces of these radiant girls.

"My favorite part of being here," another young woman said, "is our Christmas parties. Every year during Christmas, we host a party and invite all the girls from the bars to come, so we can give them presents and show them love."

One of the staff members explained, "We pay the bar owners a fee for any of the girls who want to come. It's the only time of year when they can receive. People are always taking from them."

The girls were excited to show me the rest of the house. When we went upstairs, the gentle one, who talked about the love of God, walked with me.

"What are you passionate about?" I asked.

"I make art," she said excitedly. "Want to see?"

"Absolutely!" I said.

She led me over to her collection of drawings and held one up for me to see, smiling with pride.

"That is gorgeous. You are a talented artist."

"Thank you," she said with quiet confidence. She spoke like a person who had started to grasp her own worth.

I left my dinner with the survivors of Bangkok filled with hope. After all they endured, they are living with the joy of loving and being loved. They are learning the truth of their spiritual identity and purpose. Love found them in one of the most loveless places on earth.

In the past, they were told they were nothing more than sexual commodities to be consumed by men with greater power and privilege. Now, they were preparing for college and spoke with excitement about their dreams for the future.

As I watched the sunrise over Bangkok the next day, I could see that the light within these young survivors was far fiercer than the violence that was forced on their bodies.

EMOTIONAL JUSTICE

Justice has many forms and faces. I believe in accountability for our actions, including criminal justice for those who enact violence against women and girls. Yet I also know we cannot wait for criminal justice to finally take back our power.

When the vast majority of rapists will never spend a day in jail, we have to create our own justice each day as we work toward the long-term cultural healing and political change necessary for a more compassionate world. When a survivor reclaims her worth, moves toward her dreams, shares her art, finds her community, and expresses her unique path to leadership, that is justice, too. As a global movement of survivors, we are in desperate need of more expansive visions of justice, visions that center on our healing and liberation.

When I explored how I wanted to create my own justice, I discovered several meanings for the word that opened up my vision of what is possible. One meaning of "to do justice" is "to appreciate properly." This led me to envision justice as a form of radical appreciation for survivors, their stories and their lives. I was also drawn to another layer of meaning.

To "do justice" can also mean "conformity to truth." Part of justice for survivors is living in accordance with the truth of their own nature, untamed by the lies they have been told about who they are. This kind of emotional justice is deeply interior. It can ultimately inspire a survivor to fight for social or criminal justice, but it begins within.

My understanding of identity is that it is both a remembrance and an unfolding process of creation. Through recovery we reclaim and re-create ourselves. Emotional justice gives us a way to honor who we have been and who we choose to be in the world. It restores our agency.

We no longer have to wait for someone else to be punished, so we can finally feel free. Pressing criminal charges against perpetrators may be part of a survivor's healing path, but it is *her* decision. Emotional justice gives us the space to determine what is right for our specific circumstances and path to recovery.

One archaic meaning of just is "faithful to the original." This captivated me. I imagined a form of emotional justice where we are devoted and loyal to the original identity and worth of a survivor, where we recognize and honor the Divine within her.

One way to look at justice in a situation is to ask, "After all a survivor has endured, what does *she* deserve?" When we witness injustice, we are often quick to focus on what we think the perpetrator deserves. There is a time and place for that. But what a survivor deserves must also be included in our definition of justice.

She deserves nothing less than complete reverence and support to make her own decisions.

In the future, we may design more opportunities for what is called restorative justice through community-based interventions. I trust Survivor Leaders will continue to ignite revolutionary conversations for gender reconciliation. At this moment, my focus is on helping women and girls live the truth of their unconditional worth.

From this place of emotional freedom, they can decide how they want to address their perpetrators. Devoting ourselves to a deeply personal experience of justice through inner healing and self-compassion prepares the way for collective accountability.

THE GIFTS OF PHNOM PENH

Sometimes hope comes in the small ways we can help and provide for those who are hurting. Yes, survivors want systemic social change, and we want perpetrators to be held accountable for their actions. But social justice work takes on many forms, and some days the gift we are called to give is simple and intimate.

These small gestures of kindness help create a more compassionate world. These choices are essential to holding on to hope because they remind us that we are not powerless in the face of injustice.

I may not be able to end all human trafficking and gender violence across the earth in my lifetime, but I can end it *one person at a time* by giving a single survivor hope. I see this truth every time I am invited into a shelter or crisis center. I witness the ways women and men choose to be gentle and brave by meeting the real, practical needs of those who are vulnerable.

During my trip to Southeast Asia, I visited a safe house for survivors of child sex trafficking in Phnom Penh, Cambodia. I sat in a circle with twelve children of various ages as the translator facilitated our conversation. Several of the teen girls knitted as they talked. One said, "I knit because it helps me stay calm."

Several elderly house moms showed the girls warmth and affection, laughing at their jokes and helping them with their knitting. Then the girls showed us the rooms where they slept and studied. They were happy to have a safe space, nourishing food, and loving community.

The home was simple, but it was lifesaving. Social workers, donors, house moms, advocates, therapists, cooks, teachers, security guards, and dance instructors each gave the gift they could give, so these little ones could have a place of refuge. Their contributions did not end all violence, all systemic oppression, all human trafficking, but it ended it for these valuable little girls.

As I talked with different girls about their life at the shelter, I noticed a five-year-old girl had fallen asleep right beside me. Curled up by my legs, she breathed deeply, finally safe to rest, her tiny hand curved into a loose fist with gold bracelets around her wrist. Her bangles were just like the ones Khurshida gave me. As I watched her sleep, I saw another sister I would never forget.

NOW I LIVE

The prosecuting attorney for the Texas Attorney General's Office asked me to support two teen girls in court as they testified for a federal trial in Austin, Texas. On their first day at court, I met the girls, who were fifteen and seventeen at the time.

The younger one, Lily, was outspoken and sassy. The older one, Kayce, was more melancholy and reserved, with gentle, blue eyes.

We waited at the courthouse for several days before they were allowed to testify. The wait was excruciating for them. They knew the man who trafficked them across several states was in the courtroom, trying to convince the judge and jury that the girls "wanted to work" for him when he drugged them and forced them to have sex with up to ten buyers a day.

As the defense tried to blame the girls and minimize the role of their pimp, I was in a side room trying to help them stay grounded. I told them I was a survivor as well and they could ask me any questions they wanted about my recovery. They both wanted to know what happened to me and how I got out.

"I was seven and trafficked by my nanny while my mom was in the hospital. It ended when she finally came home."

"What happened to him?" Lily asked.

"I don't know. He left. I was too young to understand what happened to me."

"So you never got justice?"

"No. I had to create my own justice."

When her turn came to testify, Lily said, "Where am I going to look? I don't want to look at him."

"I'm going to sit right in front of the witness stand, and if you start to feel overwhelmed you can just look up at me," I said. "Also, the attorney may try to lead you to say something you don't want to say. If you don't know how to respond, say, 'Can you please repeat the question?' to buy yourself some time. Be honest. You've got this."

As we walked toward the courtroom, Lily turned to me and said, "Brooke, I am doing this for myself, but I am also doing this for you, because you never got any justice."

"You are so brave," I said, smiling, with tears in my eyes.

Both Lily and Kayce were articulate and courageous on the stand. They spoke clearly about their experience, even when the defense attorney tried to lead them away from the truth.

As a result of their testimony, the solid work of the lead investigator, and the skillful strategy of the prosecuting attorney, their trafficker was sentenced to fifteen years in federal prison without parole.

Kayce came back to Austin to visit me about a year after the trial. When I opened my door, she threw her arms around me.

"I missed you!" she exclaimed.

"I missed you, too, sweetheart," I replied.

"Look! I got a new tattoo," she said.

"Let me see."

I looked at her inner arm, and in black script her tattoo said, "I Survived, Now I Live."

"I love it," I said.

"I survived so much. I am *living* now," she said.

"Yes, you are. I am so proud of you," I replied.

WOMEN'S WORTH

After I spoke on the 2015 Grammys, Lady Gaga performed with a group of sexual assault survivors at the Academy Awards. Mainstream awards shows were finally addressing violence against women and girls.

In 2016, I was invited to the Capitol to hear members of the House of Representatives read the victim impact statement from the Brock Turner rape case. It was the first time in US history that a survivor's impact statement was read into the *Congressional Record*.

Men and women, Republicans and Democrats, joined together to honor the experience of one sexual assault survivor who spoke with searing honesty and raw power about her rapist and the aftermath of the violence he perpetrated against her.

Hearing her gripping words echo in the House, through the voices of both men and women, signaled a significant shift for me. It felt like a sign of what was coming our way. Although the judge in the case did not hold Turner accountable for the gravity of his crime, sentencing him to a paltry three months in jail, the voice of the unidentified survivor reverberated across America until it reached legislators on the Hill.

In 2017, I walked with the Women's March in Austin with more than thirty thousand men and women, taking a stand for an end to sexism and misogyny. The collective march mobilized millions for what became the single largest protest in our nation's history. The explosion of the #MeToo movement, originally founded by activist Tarana Burke, followed as Harvey Weinstein and other media industry giants were toppled from their thrones, including Carl Ferrer, chief executive officer of Backpage, who pleaded guilty to sex trafficking charges.

In isolation, each of these events might not appear significant enough to signal a new era for championing women's worth. But when viewed together, the pattern is clear. Women and their male allies have spoken: "Time's up."

Ten years ago, child sex trafficking was not addressed in a comprehensive way in the mainstream media or taken seriously by many policy makers. Now it has become a national priority.

We used to be invisible. Now we are publicly identified, united, and organized. As more survivors share their stories and lead the movement, we find each other and design our own strategies for ending abuse and human trafficking. One life at a time.

chapter twelve

God of Little Girls

Returning to the Divine Feminine

I am praying to the god of little girls.
I am praying she will mend this world.

RECOVERY IS SOUL RETRIEVAL. It is a process of calling back parts of the soul and psyche that split off through trauma. In various traditions, healers and teachers guide wounded souls through ceremony to support this reclamation. They call on spiritual allies, including plant medicine, sacred songs, the elements of nature, and divine healing power.

In essence, the rituals are designed to help these split-off parts of a person's energy and consciousness to feel safe and loved. Ceremonies vary depending on the tradition of the healer and the needs of the one seeking help.

In psychological terms, the journey of soul retrieval is similar to integration, a way of connecting with the different parts of our being, offering each part compassion and welcoming these pieces of our humanity to come home.

At the beginning of my recovery, I read a transformative book called *Stranger in the Mirror: Dissociation, the Hidden Epidemic*, by Maxine Schnall. In her groundbreaking work, Schnall highlights a spectrum of dissociation and how we can begin communicating internally with parts of ourselves that need compassion and comfort.

Around this time, I also discovered the practices of indigenous healers who created ceremonies for soul retrieval. Although at first glance the worldviews of Western psychology and indigenous spirituality appear extremely different, they both articulate the importance of reconnecting with lost parts of our being.

At the time I discovered these practices, I was struggling with severe depression, dissociation, and PTSD. I did not know how to heal myself, but this guidance illuminated what I felt deep within: a soul loss, a splitting off from my body and from all life. Splitting helped me survive, but it also made me feel hollow and lonely, as if I were in perpetual mourning.

There was no rite of passage or ceremony to mark or honor what happened to me. There was no acknowledgment and no closure. There was no community that witnessed my loss and grieved with me in a way that allowed me to release the past and come home to my body.

I was not able to fully apply what I learned about integration and soul retrieval when I first encountered these ideas, but the books I read and healers I met planted a seed in me, an understanding that another way was possible.

THE TEMPLE AND THE FLAME

Therapy and Somatic Experiencing helped me to process and integrate my experiences in a way that made it safe for me to finally call my soul back to myself: all my power and energy, all my gifts and knowledge. Although I eventually met and worked with holistic bodyworkers, when I was ready to begin the process of soul retrieval, I created ceremonies on my own.

Somatic Experiencing helped me come to a place of peace by releasing the neurobiological impact of trauma and provided a strong foundation for my recovery. The next step was acknowledging the spiritual impact of my trauma and learning how to listen to the voice of my soul. The repeated sexual violence and torture taught me it was not safe to be here.

Many survivors describe the feeling of leaving their bodies during abuse and near-death experiences, as if they are hovering over the body and watching from above. Survivors may even create alternate worlds and hiding places where their abusers cannot find them.

I created many of these worlds as a child: soothing, beautiful places with clear water and gentle animals. Psychologists call this dissociation. Indigenous healers call this soul loss. My experience included both elements: psychological dissociation *and* a sense of my soul splitting off and leaving my body.

For survivors of abuse and complex trauma, we can experience a soul loss that feels like a kind of spiritual dissociation. It's as if the core flame of our humanity cannot burn brightly in the physical realm, so we hide it away for safekeeping. This feels deeper than a mere neurobiological reaction.

I envision each of us as a temple holding a sacred flame within. Our body and brain form the temple, and it is important for this temple to be a safe place, protected from invasion and harm.

The temple of the body is present to be the protector of the soul flame. When the temple is invaded, the sacred fire must be hidden

177

underground. When the temple is restored and its boundaries secure, the fire can return. The soul flame cannot be extinguished, but when the temple is being harmed, our fire does not want to stay. We begin to feel diminished, depleted, and disconnected from life. We no longer burn as brightly as we once did.

I imagine soul retrieval as a reclamation of our core fire after our bodies finally feel safe. The first step is finding a therapist or healing practice to cultivate your core sense of safety, to take back and clear out your temple. Modalities such as meditation, yoga therapy, prayer, bodywork, and herbal remedies soothe the nervous system and prepare the way for your fire to return.

Once you begin to feel safe and integrate psychologically, you can create ceremonies for soul retrieval. You don't need a healer, spiritual guide, or bodyworker to perform a ritual for you. But you may want to learn from different traditions to see what feels most aligned with your spiritual path. I love learning from the traditions of other women, but I ultimately feel the most potent healing when I curate ceremonies based on my own intuition.

After taking back my temple through Somatic Experiencing and coming into significant psychological integration, I created a simple ritual to call every part of my being home. In addition to feeling safer in my body, I was making choices to honor and protect myself in my relationships by only allowing compassionate people in my life. This communicated to any hidden or lost parts of me that this life I was living, in this body, at this moment, was a place of refuge.

In my writing studio at home, I lit four white candles, one for each direction, and placed a photograph of myself as a little girl by the candle representing the north. I burned white sage, turned off all the lights, sat in the center of the circle of candles, and entered into meditation and prayer. I envisioned the fierce light of Divine Love surrounding and protecting me and invited God to help me bring back every part of my being. As I prayed, I felt led to say out loud,

I call back my power now.
I call back my power now.
I call back my power now
from every dimension, past, present and future.
I call back my power now.
I call back every part of my being,
from all times, places and people,
free and clear of anything that has been attached to me,
free and clear of any negative energies.
I call back my power now.
I dissolve any soul ties that bind me
to those who harmed me.
I close any portals that allow them to reach me.
I call back my power now.
Let the fire of your infinite love protect me
and consume all darkness that has come against me.

As I prayed, surrounded by candlelight, I could see my trafficker and all the men who abused me being cleared away with their devouring darkness and torment. Then a powerful energy entered me with such force, my body bent over to the floor and I started yelling and weeping spontaneously. My body was crying out in agony and relief all at once. Then, I saw an image of a white wolf. She felt like an angelic presence guiding me home.

This is the first time I am sharing my experience of soul retrieval. It was so potent, wild, and miraculous, I did not want to share it with anyone. Yet as I consider my recovery, I cannot exclude the spiritual realm and what I have learned about the homecoming of the soul.

Within your own spiritual tradition and worldview, I encourage you to explore what soul retrieval might mean for you. For some, it may be as simple as honoring a passion or part of yourself you feel you lost along the way. A dormant dream. A buried desire. For others, it may be a more complex ritual integrating the sacred symbols and elements that speak to you. What is essential is discovering what helps you take care of *your* body, *your* temple, and supports you to feel safe in the world, so you can honor and welcome every part of you home.

IN THE ARMS OF THE BLACK MADONNA

My soul speaks to me in images. These images come through inner visions and dreams. The most significant ones carry messages that stay with me for years. One dream I will never forget is my dream of the Black Madonna.

One night, in the early stages of my recovery, feeling heartbroken and lost, I could not stop weeping. I felt I was grieving a loss that was deeper than me and my story. It felt like an ancient, feminine wound that never healed. In a child's pose, a yoga posture of surrender and rest, I cried until I was exhausted and said out loud, "I need a God who is a mother." A couple of nights later, my prayer was answered in a dream. Here is the dream:

I am in the crypt of Chartres Cathedral underneath the labyrinth. I am kneeling in front of the Black Madonna, sobbing with my head lowered. I raise my head to look at her and cry out, "Why did you let them put you here?"

When I had this dream I didn't know there was a Black Madonna underground at Chartres Cathedral. When I looked up photographs, I saw the Madonna holding Jesus. But in my dream, she held me.

Soon after this dream, I discovered *Longing for Darkness: Tara and the Black Madonna*, by China Galland. This remarkable book helped me understand the significance of the Black Madonna as a symbol of Mother God.

Jungian analyst Marion Woodman also contributed to my interpretation of the dream through her writing on the Black Madonna as a symbol of the hidden, repressed Sacred Feminine, who is black because she has been "through the fire."

The symbol I encountered in my dream, the Black Madonna, was Mother God underground. The One who walks through the fires of transformation. The One who is hidden, but not destroyed.

This dream initiated me into a quest for the feminine face of God in many traditions, starting with Christianity and Judaism. Once I knew *how* to look, I could see her everywhere. She was Sophia, Shekinah, and the Holy Spirit. She was the Bride, the Grail, the Dove, the Wisdom of Creation.

Her face and voice may have been forced underground by religious leaders, but she was always finding ways to make herself known. She was with me.

When I cried out to encounter God as Mother and received this dream, I was trusting the voice of my soul. This trust led me deeper into the mysteries of love. I wanted to be held, and she found me there, in the womb of a cathedral, weeping in the dark.

I reclaimed and honored another part of me. A part I didn't know was missing. My soul was teaching me what no one else could teach me, the sacredness of my own female body, the holiness of the buried and forgotten, the feminine face of God.

When I cried out on my knees, weeping over the ancient wound of the banished Mother, what I was saying with each sob, each memory, each vision and dream is *I remember.*

> *I remember Her. I remember She*
> *and She. Is. Rising.*
> *I remember who I am.*
> *I remember the dismemberment.*
> *The severing and dividing of She*
> *in me.*
> *I remember everything.*
> *I remember the God of Little Girls.*

chapter thirteen

Waking the Priestess

Honoring the Sacred Within

I am learning to praise
The rich chorus of hours
& the startling gifts
a season of singing can bring.

ONE OF THE GREATEST COSTS OF abuse and exploitation is the way victims are trained through psychological coercion to betray their own nature. What is far more painful than physical violence or verbal assault is the loss of identity, a core sense of self that is safe and valued.

The suppression of the true nature through a cycle of threats and violence with intermittent rewards creates a trauma bond between the victim and perpetrator. In fact, a victim may eventually desire to be comforted by the very person who is causing their suffering.

This creates a psychological dependency on the abuser as the victim internalizes the worldview and will of the perpetrator. As revolutionary educator Paulo Freire says, "The oppressed having

183

internalized the image of the oppressor and adopted his guidelines, are fearful of freedom."

In essence, victims are not only taught to fear punishment. They are taught to fear themselves. This is true for interpersonal violence, human trafficking, religious abuse, and other forms of systemic oppression, such as racism and sexism.

We fear ourselves, and our power, because it isn't physically or emotionally safe to be who we are. After playing a role long enough, we may forget we are not the part we play in the oppressor's game. The internalization of oppression makes it difficult for victims to know who they are and what they desire.

The will of the abuser becomes their will.

In religious abuse, the abuser claims that their will is the will of God, so victims may feel that God wants them to act in ways that are contrary to their own well-being. They have to split off from their true identity to survive a hostile environment, yet this loss of self makes them vulnerable to continued control.

Once a victim is safe from external control, she can transition into a new identity as a survivor. But this is only the beginning of freedom because she still has to face the internalized oppression she carries within, the perpetrator inside her own mind.

Our Survival Self protects our truth deep within, but the Survival Self is not our soul. It is the warrior we create to protect her. The warrior is a shape-shifter. She may appear deferential and pleasing or defiant and hard.

The warrior can be whoever she needs to be to survive the war being waged around her. She is the protector of the soul and must be honored for her service. Eventually, the Survival Self can learn to set strong, healthy boundaries that keep us safe and support us in being fully expressed in the world.

THE PRIESTESS PATH

Recovery from abuse is a path of returning to and honoring our true nature. I call this the Priestess Path. Historically, a priestess was a woman who performed the sacred rites of a religion and could communicate directly with the Divine. Although women are excluded from the priesthood and formal leadership in many world religions, women have always been spiritual leaders.

The priestess is in every tradition and creates traditions of her own. Recognized or unrecognized, celebrated or vilified, she has always been there, offering soul wisdom and guidance to her community. The priestess has never stopped teaching, praying, guiding, healing, sharing her visions, dreams, and prophecies.

I see the Priestess Path as the path of the spiritual leader who trusts the voice of her soul and guides her community with untamed light. She gives the gift she is here to give and honors herself fiercely. She sees her past through the eyes of love and understands she cannot be reduced to the experiences of her life. Her soul is part of a far greater story.

In my soul story, I had to acknowledge the pain of being victimized, so I could grieve and heal. I also learned to embrace being a survivor, to value the strength and courage it took to survive. This led me to relinquish the shame I felt around the ways I survived.

The more I learned about survivorship, the more I wanted to help others heal from abuse, so I became an advocate and activist. It was not enough to bear witness with compassion. I wanted to be a part of creating change in our culture.

I gave myself fully and completely to the work of social justice and learned many lessons from my sisters. Yet after years of activism, advocacy, and supporting survivors, I felt something was missing.

I loved my community, but I was depleted and hurting. I had become so focused on transforming the world, I lost touch with parts of myself, places within my own body and soul that needed to be seen, heard, and loved.

Desperate to save others, I ignored my vulnerabilities, needs, and secret desires. I silenced the Sacred Child within me who wanted me to stop trying to rescue everyone else and finally embrace *her*. I was giving everyone else what I desired most.

It was an honor to be part of their recovery, but it was incomplete. *She* was missing. Finding her, feeling her, listening to her again ushered in a new season for me. I write this book in honor of her.

No longer struggling to find the remedy I craved, I became the priestess of resurrections, one who knows our initiations, our descents, our deaths are not the end.

The priestess is part of the lineage of Mary Magdalene, the one who grieves by the grave when she believes her Love is dead, only to see Love rise again. That invincible love becomes her message.

The priestess is the Beloved in the Song of Solomon, who after being used and abused, proclaims, "Great seas cannot extinguish love, no river can wash it away." Through her search for her Divine Lover, she discovers her own worth and declares her personal sovereignty, saying, "My vineyard is *all my own*."

The priestess is mystic poet Rabia, who survived sex trafficking and became a powerful spiritual teacher. She wrote, "'Show me where it hurts,' God said, and every cell in my body burst into tears before His tender eyes.

"He repaid me, though, for all my suffering, in a way I never wanted: The sun is now in homage to my face, because it knows I have seen God." As she offered her suffering to God, she received a powerful healing vision that transformed her life.

The priestess is Enheduanna of ancient Sumer, who wrote this radical truth about meeting with our shadow self: "The ways of the underworld are perfect." She captured the descent and ascent of a woman's soul with luminous clarity and showed that self-compassion was the secret to healing our divided psyches.

The Priestess Path is about telling the story of the soul in our own voices. It is the transition from victim to spiritual leader. In this journey of the soul, the weary slave can become the radiant queen, self-possessed and resting on her throne. Her life of fearful submission transforms into personal sovereignty.

Nothing can separate us from our true spiritual identity and purpose on this earth. We are unconditionally valuable, and our lives are unconditionally meaningful. Yet trauma can rupture our connection to this truth. For those who experience abuse, it is even more essential for us to reconnect and remember who we are.

After we secure our freedom from physical and emotional violence, the essential work of liberation revolves around identity. How do we begin to understand who we are after trauma? How do we awaken to our worth?

There are many healing keys I've collected on my Priestess Path. Four are the most essential:

Creative expression

Divine intimacy

Self-compassion

Spiritual community

Each one serves as a unifying theme to help me heal and tell my soul story. These are the specific tools I have used to remember who I am.

In the previous chapters, I shared modalities and experiences that supported my healing, particularly in the reclamation of my identity and worth. From Somatic Experiencing and meditation to creative writing and a survivor support group, I collected practices to guide me back to my inherent dignity and resilience.

It is beyond the scope of this book to share everything and every-one who supported my healing, but in the following guide you will find some of the elements I am most grateful for.

If you are on a healing path, I highly recommend you create a circle of support around you. You are not your trauma, but you may need help returning to the knowledge of your wholeness: your orig-inal, creative, joyful life force.

When you place your recovery first and commit fully to learning how to value yourself, you will receive help beyond all you could ask or imagine. Pray or meditate each day, and listen to your inner guidance for the next step on your healing path. Your soul is wise and knows exactly what you need to heal.

Be discerning and careful with anyone who claims to have the ultimate answer or solution for you. Some therapists, researchers, thought leaders, and spiritual teachers have wisdom to offer. Take what is helpful, but don't let anyone take control of your recovery.

Excellent guides will always encourage diversity of thought and encourage you to honor your own experience. There can be a form of fundamentalism in the world of recovery, just as there can be in religion.

Take your time, interview people you might want to work with, and listen to your body. You can cause yourself tremendous suffering trying to fit into someone else's program. If it's not working for you, it's not your fault. You are not a failure if someone's method is not the right fit. Be gentle with yourself.

For most survivors I've worked with, they need a personally designed recovery program, attuned to their spiritual worldview, trauma history, neurobiology, preferences, personality, and resources. I am often asked to give referrals and recommendations for recovery programs.

Some people assume it is as simple as identifying a program that addresses their core trauma. But there are many factors involved and questions that need to be asked for me to understand what might best serve a survivor.

When evaluating a particular modality for your recovery, examine the research and see if it is trauma informed and evidence based. See if you can speak to other survivors this person has worked with. As you are exploring different forms of support, ask, "Does this help me love and trust myself more fully?" There is an abundance of resources for you to explore. You are not alone.

The path of recovery can be challenging, but ultimately it is a process of discovering who you are, expressing what you need, and learning how to create what you desire in life.

Key 1: Creative Expression

As you learned from my stories of poetry, music, acting, and speaking, creative expression has been essential for my healing. In many ways, art helped save my life.

You don't have to pursue a career in the arts to benefit from the healing power of honoring your creativity. From art therapy to open mics, from women's circles to journaling, from dance to community theater productions—a vast, rich world of creative possibility is open to you. Even if you don't want to share your trauma story through art, the act of tapping into your creativity is inherently healing.

The creative process reminds you that you are far more than your trauma. You are not your painful memories. You are the artist of your life. In my work with survivors, I witness the sense of dignity and joy that flows from women valuing their voices.

Some of my mentees write poetry, and others share their photography and paintings in our survivor art shows. Give yourself permission to play with any medium that intrigues you and connect with other women on a creative path. You are already a creatrix, a force of nature. Let your art be your medicine.

Key 2: Divine Intimacy

Cultivating a daily spiritual practice is vital for recovery. It is important to pay attention to what feels sacred to you. This is deeply personal and should reflect your unique soul story. My daily spiritual practice involves prayer, meditation, breath work, journaling, dream work, and entering into dialogue with images and messages I receive during contemplative practices.

Sometimes I include spiritual texts or poems in my time of devotion. From an energetic perspective, I pour out what is in my heart, release what I need to release, and open my whole being to receive guidance. I usually close my sessions with a simple prayer of gratitude.

I adapt my rituals to the particular season I am in, as well as my needs at the time. Right now, I usually sit in front of my altar on a green velvet meditation cushion, light a decadent sandalwood candle, and focus on my breath as I mediate. At the moment, my altar has several objects that are sacred to me, including an amethyst my Grammy gave me; Palo Santo in a shell from the Pacific Ocean; carnelian from a trip to Sedona; essential oil blends with jasmine, rose, and white sage; as well as a small black statue that reminds me of my connection with the Divine Feminine.

Holding a crystal during meditation helps me stay grounded and present. Right now, rose quartz feels the most soothing. I also place fresh flowers by my altar, usually crimson roses. I pray out loud and silently, taking time to listen within. I intuitively choose mantras or scriptures or sing spontaneously, depending on what I feel wants to come through me.

When I finish, I record any insights or messages in my journal. I also draw symbols or images I see. This helps me connect to the story my soul is telling. If I remember a vivid dream, I dialogue with a character or symbol in the dream through active imagination to see what this part of my unconscious mind may want to share.

During long nature walks, I take visions and dreams with me and sing a song about what I have seen. This can help me bring it to completion.

Depending on how I am feeling, I incorporate herbs in tinctures or teas to support my process. Adaptogenic herbs like ashwagandha, eleuthero, and holy basil are wonderful for trauma survivors in the way they can both soothe and energize. I also love blending damiana, raspberry leaf, and rose petals in a tea. It's like drinking love out of a teacup.

In the evening, I often pray and meditate in an Epsom-salt bath with essential oils, flowers, or herbs. I will sip tea or have a glass of red wine by candlelight and cleanse myself of anything I need to let go of. I open myself to receive guidance as I relax in the warm water. I may pose a question and see what arises in response.

What is important is to design a daily ritual that works for you. My practices will continue to evolve with the changing needs of my body and soul. Consider setting up a sacred space in your home where you can focus on your spiritual path and connect with your inner wisdom.

A small altar with a few items you love can provide a focal point for your practice. Even lighting a candle and sitting for a brief meditation can replenish you and give you the calm you need to enjoy the rest of your day.

Key 3: Self-Compassion

Somatic Experiencing with a therapist who specializes in complex trauma, partner violence, and sexual assault helped me create a strong foundation for cultivating self-compassion. Through the process of acknowledging the messages of my body, expressing the images and emotions connected to trauma, and staying rooted in the present, I learned how to honor each part of myself.

My sessions illuminated where I needed to offer empathy to the places within where I was still hurting. As I became more integrated, I was able to connect with the Sacred Child within and guide her home.

I tried other modalities before Somatic Experiencing, but they were not effective for me. I needed a holistic, body-centered therapy in order to bring my nervous system back into balance and begin to feel safe. I encourage you to research and explore Somatic Experiencing as well as other body-centered, trauma-informed therapies.

When you are looking for a counselor, make sure they have significant expertise and training in your core trauma. I would start by contacting your local domestic violence and sexual assault crisis center. No matter when you experienced abuse, you are eligible for free counseling.

Also, many crisis centers are now serving survivors of trafficking because there is so much overlap between domestic violence, sexual assault, and sex trafficking. After your intake appointment, a caseworker will tell you what services you can receive and make a referral if you need additional support.

If you have the financial resources to pay for therapy, your local crisis center may still be the best place for you to begin because they typically have the most training and experience to connect you with help.

When seeking a therapist, make sure they are licensed, so you know there is accountability for their therapeutic practice and they will be held to an ethical standard. Interview them to ask what modalities they use and what a course of treatment will look like. In addition to Somatic Experiencing, many women I've worked with say that EMDR (Eye Movement Desensitization and Reprocessing) has been helpful for them.

Well-intentioned "healers" and "spiritual counselors" who are not equipped to work with complex trauma can actually retraumatize you. They may not fully understand how to work gently and effectively with the neurobiology of trauma.

If you are working with a spiritual mentor or teacher, make sure there are clear boundaries. Someone who has studied theology, for instance, may have encouraging spiritual insights, but they are not necessarily trained to help you process and integrate your trauma.

Another powerful piece of cultivating self-compassion is identifying your desires and creating your love story with life. Therapy is important, but it is not there to consume your existence. It should support the exploration of your desires.

Simple exercises like writing out your desires each day and fulfilling one desire each week can help you shift your focus from past pain to present pleasure. Offer gratitude as you see your desires fulfilled. More will follow.

Writing letters of compassion to yourself teaches you how to relate to your struggles with greater tenderness. I have sent myself love letters from all over the world and mailed them home, so I could open and read them aloud. In each one, I said what I most needed to hear during a painful time of my life. It was a way to comfort, soothe, and celebrate the parts of me that have overcome so much.

Other forms of support that have helped me deepen in self-compassion and self-care include:

- **Yoga nidra**, often called gentle or restorative yoga
- **Craniosacral therapy and myofascial release**: therapeutic techniques that release trauma from the body

- **Naturopathic medicine**: working with a holistic doctor on supplements, herbs, and foods to support my mood, energy, and mental clarity based on my blood work and genetic testing
- **Mindful movement in nature**, such as walking and swimming
- **Spending time with animals**, such as equine therapy and cuddling with my pup

There are many rich ways for you to deepen your practice of self-compassion.

Key 4: Spiritual Community

For most of my life, I've felt like a spiritual misfit. I was a mystic in a traditional religious community. I could see poetry, archetypes, and symbols where others saw only literal doctrines. I carried dreams and visions in my heart that did not conform to claims made in my childhood churches.

Yet everything I experienced felt connected to the lavish compassion taught by Christ. This was deeply confusing for me. I knew the God of Love, yet those who led ministries and claimed to speak for him perpetuated misogyny in his name. My experience of religious abuse through my trafficker only amplified this confusion and pain.

They made me feel that if I left their version of the church, I was abandoning God. After exploring other religions and spiritual practices, I determined that my path was the path of the mystic and it was not my responsibility to convince anyone of the validity of my devotion. I didn't want to convert to another religion. I wanted to be free.

I learned to listen to the voice of my soul because she has a path of her own. I let this voice of love within guide me to the places, people, stories, and ceremonies that made me feel divinely connected. I craved spiritual community where a diversity of spiritual perceptions and experiences would be honored.

I did not find this in a single location: a church, a temple, or other house of worship. I found community in intimate soul talks with friends, small circles of women sharing their inner visions, coffee dates where we passionately discussed many wisdom traditions.

I have benefited from guides who practice Buddhist meditation, others who honor the cycles of the seasons through earth-based ceremonies, as well as women like my mom, who follow Christ and his Way. This is not to say that all paths are the same. They are not. But I believe all human beings are valuable and loved. They deserve to be heard when they name their experience of the sacred.

I am still learning how to name my own relationship with the sacred without the fear of being judged, ridiculed, or shamed. No one who claims to represent God can ever separate me from Divine Love. My prayer in Paris, weeping by the statue of Saint Teresa of Avila, was answered.

Wherever you are spiritually, I encourage you to speak to people you can be honest with about your struggles and doubts, your inner visions and dreams, the ways your soul is speaking to you right now.

That may begin with one friend who also wants to heal and grow spiritually. It may be a recovery group or women's spirituality circle. It could be a weekly meditation class with teaching and discussion. The important part is that you have others to walk with you and support you.

Pay attention to the spiritual books, practices, or conversations that intrigue you. You don't have to abandon everything you've once believed, but you can give yourself permission to explore, question, and see what resonates as truth.

As my meditation teacher in Boulder said, "If it's useful, use it." Remember, you are the spiritual authority in your life. Never give away your power to a leader or teacher. A loving spiritual teacher will never ask you to conform to their ideology, but will support your own process of inquiry as they share their wisdom. It is inspiring to learn from others, but trust yourself and look for communities that deepen that trust.

I host retreats for survivors, and I also attend retreats as a way to be in community with other women devoted to a spiritual path. Intentional solitude for contemplation is essential for me. Yet it is easy for me to fall into a pattern of emotional isolation without telling anyone about what is really happening in my inner world.

Spiritual community keeps me connected, grounded, and rooted in love. It is a powerful antidote to the lies we are told through abuse. Our soul friends remind us who we are when we start to forget.

I PRACTICE SEVERAL DAILY rituals to keep me in a mindset of sacred moments, including prayer, meditation by my altar, and journaling. One of my favorite mantras to say out loud while focusing on my breath is this: *"I am rooted and grounded in love."* I say this aloud while taking deep breaths until I begin to feel this truth reverberating in my body.

Another mantra I love is,

I am safe.
I am sacred.
I am whole.
I am free.

When I want to affirm my inner freedom, I recite this passage from the Gospel of Mary Magdalene:

That which oppressed me has been slain.
That which encircled me has vanished.
My craving has faded and I am freed from my ignorance.

As far as prayer, one common prayer I open with after I light a candle on my altar is,

I take refuge in you now
and surrender to your care.

If I am struggling emotionally, I may also add,

Liberate me from my suffering
and the root of my suffering.
Guide me to what I need
for complete liberation and healing.

Then I focus on my breath and listen within to see if guidance arises. After meditation, I transition to my desk to write in my journal. My journal is the place I ask for additional Divine guidance, identify my desires, explore my dreams from the previous night, write out questions, and listen to my soul voice.

Sometimes it looks like a conversation, sometimes a poem, a love letter, or an abstract map of words and symbols. This is a space for my soul to speak and honor my inner wisdom. Occasionally, I will write, "What do I need to know? I am listening." This signals that I am open and willing to receive whatever needs to come through me.

My mantras, prayers, rituals, and other spiritual practices change with the seasons. What resonates with me as I write this may not next year. So, I will not suggest that you take on my practices as your own unless they feel healing for you. What is important is for you to trust yourself and allow yourself to play with your own sense of the sacred.

If I am feeling internal resistance or disconnected from my Source, I pray,

> *I release all fear and shame to you*
> *and open myself to receive your lavish grace.*
> *Thank you for making your love known to me.*
> *Draw me deeper into the mystery of love.*

Healing is not a defined, straight line. It is an intricate spiral, like a labyrinth, leading us closer and closer to our soul center.

Mystic poet Rabia once wrote, "Dear Sisters, whatever happens in this life is bringing us closer to God." After being sold into a brothel as a child and enduring a lifetime of abuse, she gained her freedom and taught her community about the healing power of finding love within. Her resilience was miraculous. It was nourished by her devotion to the Divine and honoring the truth of her soul.

During a retreat in Sedona, surrounded by vistas of deep orange-red rocks, I entered a labyrinth made of stones set in a spiral. As the sun set over the mountains, I felt drawn there to release an old story, a script about who I am that no longer served me.

It was the story of the slave, the story of the woman who was exploited, abused, and oppressed.

I intuitively understood that I could release the energy of that story into the earth, the powerful carnelian-colored rock formations pulsing beneath my feet.

I saw an image of a black jaguar with gold eyes prowling beside me, as if she were guiding me back to the truth. With each step I took, closer to the heart of the labyrinth, I spoke aloud the names and old identities I was choosing to release. When I reached the center, I could feel all the pain rushing from my head, down through my legs and feet, into the red ground.

As soon as this suffering left my body, a new song entered through my feet and rushed to my throat. With this rush of energy, a word came to me: *sovereignty*. I sang my way out of the labyrinth into a richer experience of sovereignty over my own life.

The word *sovereignty* holds many layers of meaning, but here is one I embraced that night as pink and gold light spread across the sky: *freedom from outside control*. I know what it feels like to be treated as someone else's property or possession. I know what it is like to be used, put on display, and disposed of. I also know the more subtle erasure of silencing or sacrificing parts of myself to please others.

Yet through my recovery, I discovered the path to sovereignty by choosing to honor and protect what belongs to me. I cultivate my own garden, my own sacred ground. I choose self-possession. I finally belong to myself.

This sovereignty is possible for each of us. It is our birthright. It is our way home.

In this moment, I am envisioning you surrounded by a beautiful, untamed light, completely supported and gently guided to everything you need to heal and thrive. Trust the voice of your soul. She will help you remember how to come home.

As you take the next step in your recovery, I offer this poem as a blessing. May you always know you are worthy of love.

LOVE LETTER TO A SURVIVOR

Are you willing to treasure yourself,
to pleasure yourself in the sacred way?

Are you willing to befriend your breath
and reverence your own radiance?

Are you willing to feel what you must feel
if you surrender all defenses?
Fear will leave you famished.
Take refuge in kindness,
so what you need may feed you.

In the stillness, there is an entrance.
Only you hold the key.

Wherever you may be,
this moment is a passageway to peace.

You are not a sickness
to be cured, but a mystery
& miracle unfolding.

It is safe to let go of your striving.
You already possess
the deep knowing you need.

Listen to your hunger.
Let it be your teacher.
What are you always reaching for?

Last night I found God
behind my breast
And I want you to meet her.

When you hear my voice in the river
may the Divine remind you
of the beauty you are.

PART THREE

A Healing Guide for Survivors

Cease this excavation.
Lay those rusted tools aside.
You worship at the altar of your past
& it makes you weep.
Keep a new vigil.
Rise & make love to the light.

IN THIS SECTION OF THE BOOK, I offer journal prompts, discussion questions, and exercises to support your healing path. Each part of the guide connects to a core theme in my own recovery story. If you want to dive deeper into this exploration of spiritual identity and self-worth, I encourage you to dedicate a new journal to the reclamation of your untamed light. May this exploration feed your soul fire and unleash your luminosity into the world.

CHAPTER ONE: WORTHY OF LOVE

1. When do you feel most connected to your worth?
2. What was a moment in your life when you felt devalued by someone else?

3. What message did they communicate through their actions? What is the truth you choose to claim instead?

4. What would you allow yourself to do if you knew you were unconditionally valuable?

5. Write yourself a love letter. Speak to a part of you that has been hurt in the past. Tell her what she needs to hear most.

6. Place your letter in an envelope and address it to yourself. Mail the message, and when it arrives, open your letter with loving intention. Read aloud your words of compassion to this part of you. Save the letter along with others you may want to send in the future. Return to these words when you need to be reminded how to treat yourself with kindness.

CHAPTER TWO: UNDERWORLD GIRL

1. What is the story you need to tell?
2. What is the story you are afraid to tell?
3. When did you learn it wasn't safe to be yourself?
4. What keeps you silent?
5. Who would you be if you surrendered your shame?
6. Fill in the blank: I never told anyone that _____.

CHAPTER THREE: THE ARTIST AND THE DESTROYER

1. How can you honor your inner artist?
2. How are you already expressing your creativity?

3. Have you ever told yourself you are not "an artist"? Is that belief serving you?

4. We are all born inherently creative. What forms of art or creative expression would you give yourself permission to explore, if it didn't have to be "perfect"?

5. Do you have an inner critic or inner abuser? Who taught you to speak to yourself this way?

6. Write down all the messages of your inner critic or inner abuser, and burn them in a ceremony. Thank your critic for trying to protect you, and let this part of you know that another way is possible. You have the power now to set boundaries out of self-compassion, instead of hiding your truth out of fear.

Voice Mantra

Create a mantra to affirm the power and worth of your voice. Let this be rooted in your deepest spiritual truth, not something that feels artificial or forced. Repeat this mantra out loud or internally during meditation or throughout your day.

I like to recite my mantras out loud during times of prayer and meditation at my altar, focusing on my breath. This signals to my body and mind that I am opening myself to deeper healing.

There are many different kinds of breath work and sitting meditation practices. I encourage you to experiment and explore with various techniques until you discover what feels natural for you. Sometimes I focus on an object on my altar, such as my grandmother's amethyst or the candle flame. This helps me stay focused. Other times I close my eyes and travel within. Here are some mantra suggestions to play with:

- I am learning to value my voice.
- I deserve to be heard.
- My truth is power.
- My voice heals.
- It is safe to speak my truth now.
- My truth sets me free.

CHAPTER FOUR: A SOUNDTRACK FOR SURVIVAL

1. Name a few of the poets, artists, singers, and storytellers whose voices deeply resonate with you. What quality do you see in their work?
2. What are some ways you can honor these qualities within yourself?
3. Create an altar to honor your voice and creative power. Consider including photographs or symbols you connect to these voice muses.

Some of my muses include Mary Magdalene, Billie Holiday, Rabia, and Frida Kahlo. Each one of these women carries powerful soul medicine for me. They embody the wild truth I want to share in my own life. They all overcame trauma to share their untamed light with the world.

In their work I see passion, courage, and beauty. For instance, Patron Saint of Untamed Women Billie Holiday boldly sang about her experience of domestic violence. She survived exploitation in a New York brothel as a young teen and became a legendary voice, channeling her pain into power through her sultry, soulful songs. This is the kind of alchemy that reminds me why I want to create.

Healing is learning to accept and offer grace to all parts of our experience. Art is spacious enough to hold it all: the images of dreams, the mystery, the renegade ache. The creative process reminds me that I am not a problem to be solved.

I may be in pain, but I am not that pain. I am the compassionate witness, and my life is far more than suffering. It is not denial to intentionally shift my focus and find what I can celebrate. It is devotion to possibility. That is what poetry and music give me.

CHAPTER FIVE: MARY MAGDALENE BLUES

1. What sacred stories, texts, or myths resonate with you?
2. What religious stories have you been told that evoke fear or shame?
3. What is sacred to you?
4. When do you feel a sense of the sacred?
5. How can you create space to give more of your time and attention to what feels sacred to you?

There are many lessons that have been hidden from us as a result of the assault on the Sacred Feminine. But one lesson is this: We have always been the Beloved. We have always been worthy. Being born female is not a sin. We are fiercely fashioned in the image of the Divine. We are not the toxic scripts we have inherited through violence and erasure. We are sacred, whole, and free.

As I share in my story about singing in the jail, I believe in the power of women's sacred stories to heal and restore us. I sang a song about Mary Magdalene for incarcerated women because for centuries religious teachers have misrepresented who she is. I knew they could relate to the ways she has been falsely defined.

She was labeled a prostitute or merely a "repentant sinner." Yet the traditional canon and Gnostic Gospels do not support this. Her wisdom as a spiritual leader and teacher was buried. Her voice was silenced. She was reduced to a myth that stripped her of her full humanity. Her role as Beloved and witness to the death and resurrection of her Love has been obscured.

In the Gospel of Mary Magdalene, the soul says, "That which oppressed me has been slain. That which encircled me has vanished. My craving has faded and I am freed from my ignorance." The greatest ignorance is the ignorance of our own true nature. Our sacred stories help us remember who we are.

CHAPTER SIX: HOUSE OF LIES

1. Where are you divided? What will it take to come home to your wholeness?
2. Are you willing to witness and embrace all parts of you?
3. Have you experienced religious abuse or shaming through religion? If so, how has this impacted your sense of the sacred and your core spiritual identity?
4. Have you been told you have to suppress or silence your humanity to please God or others?
5. If you are part of a religion, do you feel free to fully honor and express your humanity? If not, how can you bring more of your truth and voice into shaping your religious experience?

6. If you haven't been shamed through religion, you may have felt pressure to slave for perfection. Perfectionism is the new religion for many women, even those who are not a part of organized religion. What would you allow yourself to feel, know, and create, if you didn't have to be "perfect"? How can you let love in by allowing yourself to be beautifully human?

7. We have all inherited the narratives of patriarchy and internalized our own oppression on some level. For women who have experienced gender violence, this narrative is anchored in our bodies. It is also a form of ancestral knowledge from generation after generation of inherited trauma. Freedom begins with making the invisible visible. What house of lies were you born into?

8. If you want to document your discoveries, draw a simple rendering of your inner house and write out the core agreements that hold it together. Allow yourself to feel what it would be like to leave it behind. What comes up for you? Trust your process. Do you feel led to visualize dissolving or burning the house after you leave?

When I want to energetically release a spiritual agreement, false narrative, or old identity that no longer serves me, I write it out on a piece of paper and burn it in my ceramic fireproof bowl under the full moon or another day that feels aligned with my intention. I then either bury or release the ashes into the wind, praying aloud, "I release this to you. Thank you for your healing."

If there is a specific spiritual truth I want to claim and embody, I stand barefoot on the earth and speak this into being. I occasionally add a mantra to close, such as "I call back my power now from all times, places, and people" to reclaim the energy that belongs to me and may have been split off through old patterns. The key for me is not in exactly what I say, but the intention I hold and my undivided devotion to freedom.

CHAPTER SEVEN: TAKE REFUGE

1. Have you ever been in a physically or emotionally abusive relationship?
2. If so, how did this impact you? Did you lose or silence parts of yourself?
3. In what ways did you try to change your partner or abuser? Did you try to "help" this person or "heal" them?
4. What did this relationship cost you?
5. What needs and desires do you want to reclaim for your own well-being?

All of the survivors of sexual assault, domestic violence, and human trafficking I've worked with struggle with codependency. Without support for our recovery, we are easily pulled into the role of the caretaker, martyr, or rescuer. We've been trained through our trauma that our needs and desires don't matter. But we want love, so we form bonds through caretaking.

We often place the welfare of others above our own and lose connection to our truth. We struggle with low self-worth, yet find a sense of identity and purpose in taking responsibility for those who are struggling in ways that end up causing us harm.

The person we try to "help" might be an addict, suffering from mental illness, or refusing to take responsibility for their life in some way—for instance, their financial security. Our intentions are good: we want to save the world (one dysfunctional relationship at a time). Empathy is our superpower. We can read people and intuit their needs as soon as we walk into a room.

When it comes to dating, we can mistake compassion for someone's struggles, for the healthy love that flows from mutual respect and real intimacy. Codependency can *feel* like closeness, but ultimately it is a merging between two people rather than separate individuals connecting. The "me" is lost to "we." Boundaries collapse. The drive to "save" mimics love, but it ends in destruction. The codependent partner will always be sacrificed.

There are twelve-step groups, recovery circles, and insightful books addressing codependency. What most helped me was reading literature on these dynamics and bringing my experiences into my therapy sessions.

I looked at the ways my emotional and physical boundaries were violated in the past, so I could process the original trauma and create the boundaries that support healthy intimacy now. Becoming conscious of codependent patterns has also helped me identify red flags for unhealthy behaviors much quicker in my dating life.

CHAPTER EIGHT: SEARCHING FOR PERSEPHONE

1. Imagine your life on two time lines. One is the time line of trauma with all the major losses, severe struggles, and painful

events. Another is the time line of your joy, with all the significant moments of success, celebration, and connection. Draw two horizontal lines to depict this, and mark where each major event falls.

I started with my trauma line and added what I call my four initiations (human trafficking, two brain injuries, and domestic violence), but you can write down as many events as you want. I also added four highlights on my joy line.

2. Now imagine that each time line becomes one strand in your double helix to become your Story DNA. Joy and pain join in a unified dance, a meaningful, cohesive narrative of being fully you, fully human. You don't have to deny your trauma or silence your inner ecstasy. The truth is we are not a particular version of our story. We are authors possessing the power to embrace all we have experienced through the dance of our Story DNA.

CHAPTER NINE: DESCENDING WITH INANNA

1. What have you silenced? What have you buried away? What have you banished to the dark?

2. What message does your anger have for you? How can you honor your anger?

3. Write a letter to your anger, and thank her for all she does to protect you and guide you to your truth.

4. Anger is a signal that you want something to change. For what change is your anger asking? This may be both a personal life change and a collective social change.

5. Make an anger playlist and dance through your anger. Extra points if you sing along.

CHAPTER TEN: UNTAMED LIGHT

1. Finish this sentence ten times: Power is _____.
2. Finish this sentence ten times: Powerful people _____.
3. Notice what beliefs come up about power. What do you see? Identify any negative beliefs you may have about power that keep you from stepping into your own.
4. Write down three leaders you admire. What are the values you associate with these leaders? These are your core leadership values.
5. How do you want to lead in your own community? Who do you want to serve?
6. What changes do you want to see in your community? How can you lead by example by embodying these changes in your own life?

CHAPTER ELEVEN: CREATING BEAUTIFUL JUSTICE

1. What does justice mean to you?
2. What would Beautiful Justice look like in your recovery?
3. In what ways have you already taken back your power?
4. What are some new ways you feel led to express your creative power in the world?

5. What desires and dreams do you want to fulfill as part of your Beautiful Justice?

6. Take one action to support your unique definition of Beautiful Justice each week. Remember, radical self-care is revolutionary.

CHAPTER TWELVE: GOD OF LITTLE GIRLS

1. Envision your body as a temple and your soul as a beautiful flame. In what ways have you hidden and protected your flame?

2. Many survivors experience dissociation or what indigenous healers call "soul loss." What parts of yourself do you feel you have lost or disconnected from?

3. What dreams or desires have you neglected as you have focused on survival? How can you take one step toward a lost dream today?

4. How does your Survival Self show up? Is she pleasing and deferential? Is she angry and aggressive? Does she try to keep you safe by becoming what others want to see?

5. Write a letter of gratitude to your Survival Self for all the ways she has protected you. Let her know that she is a valued part of you, but she doesn't need to hide you anymore.

6. Have you seen a glimpse of your Sacred Child? How does she show up for you? In dreams, desires, or playfulness? In body pain, grief, or the hunger for safety and love?

7. If you struggle with flashbacks from childhood abuse, imagine yourself walking into those memories, taking the hand of your Sacred Child, and guiding her to a place of refuge. Ask

this part of you: What do you need? What would feel good? Remind her she is safe now and you are willing to listen to her truth. Write down any messages that come through.

CHAPTER THIRTEEN: WAKING THE PRIESTESS

1. Do you relate to the priestess archetype?
2. In what ways have you been (or would you like to be) a spiritual leader or guide to others?
3. What female spiritual teachers and wisdom keepers encourage you in your healing?
4. What is their core message? What themes do you notice?
5. If you had a chance to share your core spiritual message with the world through writing, speaking, or the arts, what would you want to share?
6. What is the truth burning inside of you?
7. What wisdom have you discovered that needs to be released?
8. Your stories carry soul medicine for you and the world. Are you willing to let yourself be heard?

Fears may arise as you move to tell your stories. Remember, there is a fire inside of you that is far more powerful than fear. Telling the truth will give you the courage you need to continue. Give yourself permission to begin: one word, one line at a time. Do not wait to *feel* brave. Speak what is true for you right now, and your bravery will rise to meet you there.

You will have your own path to discovering a wild, relentless grace that is vast enough to hold space for all of you: all your experiences, all your vulnerable, hurting, courageous, and radiant parts. When you have endured complex trauma, it is easy to constantly collect evidence for why the world is not a safe or loving place. Yet your soul is calling you deeper still.

What if there is a love that is unshaken, unbroken, a fierce compassion that only deepens when the pain comes?

The pain will come.

Will you let yourself be loved?

Will you let yourself be held and then become the compassionate witness you needed most when you were hurting?

*Y*OU ARE UNTAMED light.

Let me see how beautifully you burn.

Acknowledgments

I offer my gratitude to my mama, Mollie O'Meara Axtell, for bringing me into this wildly beautiful world, encouraging me to value my voice, and being a midwife for this book. You generously witnessed the raw stories that would become *Beautiful Justice*. Thank you for your wisdom and compassion. I would not be here without you.

Thank you to my editor, Laura Mazer, for believing in *Beautiful Justice* and guiding me through the process of refining my manuscript with grace and discernment.

I also offer my gratitude to all the women and girls who courageously shared their sacred stories with me. Your resilience, creativity, and courage inspired this book. Thank you for inviting me to be a part of your healing path.

About the Author

BROOKE AXTELL is the founder and director of She Is Rising, a healing movement for women and girls overcoming rape, abuse, and sex trafficking. Through her mentorship programs, retreats, and workshops, Brooke helps survivors thrive and become leaders. She is passionate about inspiring women to reclaim their worth and express their power to create a more compassionate world.

Brooke has spoken at the 2015 Grammy Awards, the United Nations, and the US Institute for Peace. She is a member of the Speaker's Bureau for Rape, Abuse, Incest, National Network (RAINN), the largest anti-sexual-assault organization in the United States, and an adviser for Freedom United, a global initiative to end human trafficking.

Her work as a writer, speaker, performing artist, and activist has been featured by many media outlets, including the *New York Times*, the *Los Angeles Times*, *Rolling Stone*, *Time* magazine, the *Wall Street Journal*, CNN, and *The Steve Harvey Show*. Brooke has published several award-winning poetry books and released three CDs of original music to critical acclaim.

For more recovery tools and resources for survivors visit brooke axtell.com.